THE PROMISE

José Rivera

I0139712

BROADWAY PLAY PUBLISHING INC
224 E 62nd St, NY, NY 10065
www.broadwayplaypub.com
info@broadwayplaypub.com

THE PROMISE
© Copyright 1989 by José Rivera

Cover image taken from *Mexican Masks,* University of Texas Press. Cover image design: Atelier Lebas, Los Angeles.

I S B N: 978-0-88145-678-3

First published by B P P I: April 1989
First printing this edition: November 2016

Book design: Marie Donovan
Word processing: Microsoft Word
Page make-up: Adobe InDesign
Typeface: Palatino
Printed and bound in the U S A

ACKNOWLEDGMENTS

Special thanks to: Heather Dundas, Laura Barnett, Pam Berlin, Cordelia Gonzalez, René Rivera, José Cruz Gonzalez, Yolanda Lloyd, Jerry Patch, John Glore, Ann Betancourt, Alex Colón, Jim Lewis, Max Ferra, EST's playwrights' unit, Jimmy Victor, Armando Molina, Bill Craver, Wiley Hausam, Willie Reale, Andrea Borden, and the casts, crews, and staffs of the Los Angeles Theater Center and the Ensemble Studio Theater productions.

THE PROMISE was first produced at the Los Angeles Theater Center (Bill Bushnell, Artistic Producing Director; Diane White, Producer) in Los Angeles on 12 February 1988. The cast and creative contributors were:

GUZMAN ....Shawn Elliott
ALEGRIA/PRIEST ....Julio Medina
MALINCHE/WOMAN IN SHROUD ....Maruca Medina
LILIA .... Lucy Rodriguez
LOLIN ....Diane Rodriguez
MILTON .... Nestor Serrano
CARMELO/HIBERTO ....Ray Oriel

Director .... José Luis Valenzuela
Set design ....Rosario Provenza
Costume design .... Tina Cantu Navarro
Lighting design .... Robert Wierzel
Sound design ....Jon Gottlieb
Masks & puppets design .... Cat Dragon
Original music .... Francisco Gonzalez
Dramaturg ....Halldis Hoass
Stage manager ....Jill Johnson

THE PROMISE premiered in New York at the Ensemble Studio Theater (Curt Dempster, Artistic Director), on 30 November 1988. The cast, in order of appearance, was the following:

GUZMAN .... Jaime Sanchez
LILIA .... Socorro Santiago
CARMELO/HIBERTO .... Donald Berman
1 SPIRIT PERSON .... Deborah Marcus
2 SPIRIT PERSON .... Andrea Kooharian
MALINCHE .... Kate Gyllenhaal
LOLIN/WOMAN IN SHROUD .... Ivonne Coll
MILTON .... René Moreno
PRIEST/ALEGRIA .... Yusef Bulos

Director .... David Esbjornson
Set design .... Ann Sheffield
Costume design .... Toni-Leslie James
Lighting design .... Greg MacPherson
Sound design .... Bruce Ellman
Prop design .... Peter Boles
Choreographer .... Kate Gyllenhaal
Producer .... Kate Baggott
Stage manager .... Camille Calman

CHARACTERS

LILIA, *a Puerto Rican girl of eighteen.*

GUZMAN, *her father, a superstitious old man, who looks forty.*

MILTON, *her brother, twenty-three.*

CARMELO, *her predestined husband, eighteen.*

HIBERTO, *her fiance, thirty-three. The actor doubles as* CARMELO.

LOLIN, *her neighbor and friend, thirty-nine.*

ALEGRIA, CARMELO's *father, a very old, sick man.*

PRIEST, *middle aged. The actor doubles as* ALEGRIA.

MALINCHE, *a fighting chicken played by a dancer in a mask.*

WOMAN IN SHROUD, *middle aged. The actress doubles as* LOLIN.

SCENES

ACT ONE

Prologue
Scene One—*A June morning, present day.*
Scene Two—*That evening.*
Scene Three—*That night.*
Scene Four—*Later that night.*
Scene Five—*Very early the next morning.*

ACT TWO

Scene One—*A September afternoon.*
Scene Two—*An hour later.*
Scene Three—*Later that night.*
Scene Four—*An afternoon several days later.*
Scene Five—*Continuous action.*
Scene Six—*Continuous action.*
Scene Seven—*Continuous action.*
Scene Eight—*Weeks later.*

Time: The present.

Place: The backyard of GUZMAN's *home in Patchogue, New York.*

THE PROMISE, inspired by THE DYBBUK by S Ansky, is dedicated to the memory of Jonathan Sand.

ACT ONE

Prologue

(Dark stage. Lights up on CARMELO, GUZMAN *and* LILIA. CARMELO *and* LILIA *face each other.)*

*(*LILIA *is eighteen, dark-eyed, fearless, intelligent, and pretty. She dresses like a tomboy. She has a gold cross around her neck and an odd, unnatural-looking blue flower pinned to her shirt.)*

*(*GUZMAN, *her father, is a tough, passionate, superstitious man whose true age is a mystery—maybe early forties. There isn't a grey hair on his head.)*

(Bandages cover the fingers of GUZMAN's *right hand. His factory uniform says "Lockheed" on the back and "Guzman" on the front.)*

*(*CARMELO *is* LILIA's *predestined husband: a dark, soulful, tortured young man of eighteen. He wears shabby clothes. Dust clings to him like a second skin. He holds a flower identical to hers.)*

*(*CARMELO *begins reciting a poem.)*

CARMELO: Dearest Lilia, my wife…

*(*LILIA *continues the poem.)*

LILIA: …we will die together.
And be buried apart.
And our broken bones will never embrace.
And our cold lips will never kiss.

And you will never hear
My deep declarations of love.
(She laughs: a warm, free, sexy laugh.)
But up in Heaven, our twin souls will dance,
Make love, bring new light,
And alarm the blushing angels...

CARMELO: ...your loving husband, Carmelo.

(Lights down on CARMELO *and* LILIA. *They exit.)*

Scene One

(Lights up on GUZMAN's *backyard in Patchogue, New York. Present day)*

(It's a stark, humid June morning, about 7 A M. No wind or relief from the climbing sun.)

*(*GUZMAN's *house is a post-war bungalow with big windows, a pitched roof, a porch, and some charm. The back door leads to the offstage kitchen.)*

(The backyard is surrounded by a battered picket fence.)

(On the other side of this fence, bulldozers are digging a pit which has devoured half the neighborhood. GUZMAN's *house sits unhappily at the frontier of this pit.)*

(In the yard are:)

(A hammock hanging between two leafless trees;)

(A small garden with several rows of corn, a few inches high;)

(A decrepit chicken coop laced with barbed wire;)

(A plastic statue of the Virgin Mary squashing a snake;)

(A transistor radio, attached to the statue, playing a tinny Latin melody between bursts of static;)

(and picnic benches around a lopsided table.)

(The yard could also contain a few trappings of suburban life: a rusted barbecue grill, a cracked cesspool cover, a mangled rose bush, a lawn mower, etc.)

(GUZMAN is in the garden, staring unhappily at the stunted corn.)

(He takes a knife from his pocket. He cuts the palm of his hand. His blood falls on the corn. He makes the sign of the cross as he "waters" the corn with blood.)

(LILIA enters from the house with a cup of coffee. She watches GUZMAN uneasily. Music continues.)

LILIA: ¡Café!

(GUZMAN, absorbed in his work, barely looks up as LILIA kisses him on the cheek. Music continues.)

LILIA: Pop? Why don't you ever use fertilizer?

GUZMAN: Sometimes, Lilly, you have to sneak around nature to get her to do what you want.

LILIA: Yeah? What happens when nature strikes back and gives you blood poisoning?

GUZMAN: *(Not listening)* I bet the Mafia doesn't teach you this in school. *(Showing her his bloody hand)* This is science too! And it works! This fall, we'll harvest the corn and dance at your wedding.

(Annoyed, LILIA turns off the radio.)

GUZMAN: That's what your mother told me last night—

LILIA: I'm not listening to this—

GUZMAN: That's right! I put your mother's picture under my pillow and I dreamed of her—

LILIA: Pop, don't be late for work—

GUZMAN: —and she walked right into my bedroom, gossiping about the saints—

LILIA: *(Determined)* And let me clean your hand. It's disgusting.

GUZMAN: —and she said when the corn grows, you'll get married. She said blood, *la sangre,* will *make* the corn grow—

LILIA: I'm going to clean your hand right now, Pop.

GUZMAN: She said when a girl turns eighteen, it's time to bless her parents with a grandchild.

LILIA: —Papi, you're going to get an *infection.*

(LILIA grabs GUZMAN's bloody hand and gives him the cup of coffee.)

(He looks at her darkly as she cleans his hand. He knows he can't push her too hard.)

GUZMAN: You think it's superstition, don't you?

LILIA: *(Nervous)* Ain't physics, Pop.

GUZMAN: *Digame* how come, back in Marcario, when they buried Fullano Gonzalez under a coffee bush—*the next day* the coffee beans were fatter than eggs? *(No answer)* When your mother told me that story—.

(LILIA quickly pulls away.)

LILIA: *Pop will you stop it, will you please just stop it?* We have to stop talking about Mom like this.

GUZMAN: *(Angry)* Who the hell do you—?

LILIA: I turned eighteen Monday, okay? I'm officially not a kid anymore. I can't keep thinking like a kid—

GUZMAN: Disrespect! That's all they teach you in *esse* Mafia high school!

LILIA: I respect her—I do—I'm even willing to live with the closets still full of her clothes—the house smelling like her perfume—and I don't even mind making her a plate of rice and beans—

GUZMAN: She might be hungry!

LILIA: —*but I can't keep talking about Mom like she's alive.* She's not alive. And I can't get married because you say she wants me to.

(LILIA *starts toward the house.* GUZMAN *grabs her hand.*)

GUZMAN: I'm not leaving this house looking like an old man.

(GUZMAN *sits. He drinks his coffee.* LILIA *stands behind him. With some resignation, she searches his scalp for grey hairs. This is their daily ritual.*)

GUZMAN: You're conceited. That's why you won't let me take you to the cockfights to find a *novio*.

LILIA: This isn't Marcario, Pop.

GUZMAN: *(Not listening)* You're just like tia Modesta, who thought she was the most beautiful girl in Marcario! She loved herself so much, she covered her kitchen and bathroom with a thousand mirrors so she could watch herself eat and shit.

LILIA: *(Grimacing)* Nice, Pop.

GUZMAN: And every lopsided boy in town—soon as ambition popped up between his legs—ran to her house, begged her to get married, and she said "No, baby." In her lifetime, Modesta broke the hearts of a hundred *jibaros*, six priests, and two American businessmen who heard of her great beauty in Pittsburgh.

(LILIA *can't help but laugh.* GUZMAN *always manages to disarm her. She kisses the top of his head.*)

GUZMAN: Finally, old Modesta died an ugly, dehydrated, depressing eighty-year-old virgin. A riot busted up her lonely heart every night that nobody wanted her. Every night for eighty years. *(He looks at her.)* You want to die like that?

LILIA: No.

(From far away, a bulldozer roars, digging up the earth. The sound is faint, but it grows as the play progresses.)

GUZMAN: *(Hurries to the fence and looks at the pit; the bulldozer roars.)* They're doing it again. The Mafia is digging the pit. *(To bulldozer:)* Hey! Dump *essa mierda* in your own backyard!

(GUZMAN watches, transfixed. LILIA smiles sadly.)

LILIA: Everything can't be the Mafia, Pop…

(LILIA pulls GUZMAN away from the fence.)

GUZMAN: It's them! Who else is killing our trees and animals? You never see birds anymore? The Mafia kills them and sells their songs for a profit! I swear, every tree in Patchogue is pissed off because men make this town so ugly.

(LILIA tries to make him sit, but he's still fuming.)

GUZMAN: When we moved here from Marcario and you and Milton were just kids…this was the only house in the woods that went from Sunrise Highway to the ocean. We were scared of the woods…we had respect for them…*ahora*, the Mafia can just— ppffffffft!—wipe them out like nothing.

(LILIA finally makes him sit. GUZMAN is getting worked up.)

GUZMAN: When I find Marcario and dig up my four hundred machetes and liberate Puerto Rico…the Mafia will *never* again….

(LILIA finds a grey hair and pulls it out.)

GUZMAN: …ow!

LILIA: *(Looking at the hair)* This one's white as snow.

(LILIA gives GUZMAN the hair. He inspects it. He takes a beautiful, old, gold pocketwatch from his uniform. He opens

the back of the watch, puts the hair inside, and closes the watch.)

(He puts his ear to the watch.)

GUZMAN: *Ay Dios*, Lilly! Time makes the most beautiful tick-tick-tick when it's going backwards. Keep looking. I'm going to be twenty-one again if it kills me.

(LILIA continues looking for grey hairs.)

(Suddenly, GUZMAN looks at LILIA, grabbing her hands, looking very, very sad.)

GUZMAN: Lilia, *oye!* Real love—what your mother and I have—real love has the power to swell out of the grave, find you in your best secret place, and remind you of all the promises you ever made.

(GUZMAN wipes an imaginary tear from his eye. He's moving in for the kill. LILIA knows something's up.)

GUZMAN: Poor Elena died of too much love, too much happiness! That's why she still comes back to me. That's why she can't keep her hands off me. *(Quickly)* And, like it or not, that's why she told me to tell you to marry Hiberto Muñoz.

(LILIA stops looking for grey hairs.)

LILIA: Hiberto Muñoz!? Did Patchogue run out of men?

GUZMAN: He's your mother's choice!

(Before LILIA can respond:)

GUZMAN: *And I like him!* He's an important young man who stayed single thirty-three years for you.

LILIA: Because nobody wants him! He's filthy!

GUZMAN: When I bring him over, you're going to wear a dress for him—*como una señorita...*

LILIA: I have graduation practice today—.

(She tries to leave. He stops her again.)

GUZMAN: You got a boyfriend you're not telling me about? What's his name?

LILIA: He has no name. I have no one.

GUZMAN: You better not come home one day telling me you're pregnant.

LILIA: Pregnant?! I live like a nun here!

GUZMAN: *I have a right to legitimate grandchildren!* And in this town of shadows and freaks there are men who want to take that right away from me. Remember Carmelo Alegria? I'm trying to protect you from boys like that—.

(When LILIA hears CARMELO's name, she instinctively looks at her blue flower. GUZMAN rips it from her pocket and throws it down.)

GUZMAN: Lilia, I know the Muñoz family isn't perfect. His father's a pig. His mother's a convicted felon. But they respect their heritage—they still celebrate the Epiphany! There's fame and influence in that family. People will talk about us, *mija*. What's wrong with getting a piece of that?

LILIA: *(Sad, not listening)* Don't worry, Pop. Carmelo is never coming back to me...

GUZMAN: *(Not listening)* And I swear, when old Muñoz dies, in the autopsy, they'll find his bones *stuffed* with money.

(LOLIN ALVAREZ, GUZMAN's neighbor, appears at the top of the fence.)

(Note: People can enter the yard by climbing a ladder on the other side of the fence, which makes them look as if they're standing on air. To enter, they step down onto the chicken coop and into the yard.)

(LOLIN, *a single mother of three, is a lovely, lonely woman approaching forty. She dresses to show off her body. She's clutching a bunch of letters.*)

LOLIN: They'll also find your father's puckered lips half way up the man's asshole—

GUZMAN: *(Ignoring her)* Hiberto wants to marry a virgin: that's important—

LOLIN: *(Mimicking him)* "A woman's place is in the home—with a broken leg!" Right, Guzman?

LILIA: *(Quickly)* Hi Lolly—sorry I can't stay...

(LILIA *is in the house before* GUZMAN *can stop her.*)

(LOLIN *enters the yard with a big smile and the letters.* GUZMAN *glares at her.*)

GUZMAN: You dumb bitch, I almost had her.

LOLIN: I got your damn mail again.

(GUZMAN *looks at* LOLIN *angrily—then gives her an evil smile. His personality seems to change whenever he's near this attractive woman. She's used to it: It's part of their rapport.*)

LOLIN: And take your greasy eyes off me. I feel dirty enough.

GUZMAN: *(Smiles)* All my eyes want to do...is... uncover the secret passageways of Lolin Alvarez... and...unzip the iron jacket around her heart.

LOLIN: *(Laughs)* Don't lie. I know what you wanna unzip. *(She thrusts a letter in his face.)* Here. Stop being so paranoid and get a mailbox already.

(GUZMAN *looks at the letter.*)

GUZMAN: I can't read this: It's in Spanish.

LOLIN: *(Translating)* Bruto, it says if you don't pay the Ponce Funeral Home in, let me see, thirty days...

they're gonna unbury your grandmother and send her corpse to you, C O D.

GUZMAN: I told Milton to pay this. Never trust a *pendejo* drug addict! *(He rips the letter and throws it in the chicken coop.)*

LOLIN: You better pay that. How you gonna fit a coffin back here?

GUZMAN: It's a sin how that Juan Bobo lies to me. *Milton! ¡Coño! Get your ass out here!*

(LILIA appears at the porch with schoolbooks.)

LILIA: *(Lying)* Milton's working.

GUZMAN: Don't lie. I know he's sneaking out every night. And it's not for working. It's for drugs.

LOLIN: Just keep your dead granny away from my kids. They'll eat her and I don't want them getting new diseases.

LILIA: Milton's not on drugs and *go to work.*

(LILIA starts to usher GUZMAN toward the house.)

GUZMAN: No, no, look at these hands...*bendito*...they should be counting money, not grinding magnets...

LILIA: Invest in gloves, Papi...*go*...!

(LILIA pushes GUZMAN to the door. He kisses her.)

GUZMAN: *Que Dios te bendiga. (He makes the sign of the cross over* LILIA. *To* LOLIN:*)* For you: Eh!

(GUZMAN gives LOLIN the middle finger and exits. She laughs. LILIA can finally relax. But only for a second—GUZMAN comes back in.)

(Lights change to highlight GUZMAN. Music from the radio plays.)

GUZMAN: Lockheed is killing Pedro Guzman. They don't use my true talents: my unquestioned links to

God, the Holy Ghost, and dead people. They got me
grinding magnets all day on an emory wheel 'cause
I'm a spic. Grinding magnets for electric motors for
the F-111 is not genius work. Genius work is what I
did in Marcario, when I grew the sweetest sugar cane
in Puerto Rican history. I fertilized it with Elena's
laughter.

(A blue spotlight on LILIA, *who stands up and laughs. It's a
wistful, sexy laugh mixed with melancholy.)*

GUZMAN: Before the harvest, I made my Elena stand in
the middle of the field. She let go that sweet laugh and
her voice fell on that thirsty crop like sugar! She was
my genius. She was my luck. *(He leaves.)*

(Lights to normal. Music stops. LILIA *sits on the hammock,
discouraged.)*

LOLIN: You okay?

LILIA: I just had a vision of my golden wedding
anniversary with Hiberto Muñoz. We have a family
of dwarf-children. They have big baby heads, old man
faces, and they hang on me with sticky hands, crying
"Mama, Mama, I'm hungry!" Then they eat me.

LOLIN: Sound like my kids.

LILIA: Now he's saying *Mom* wants grandchildren.
What am I supposed to say to my dead mother? No?
Maybe I won't go to college—maybe I'll stay home and
take care of him…

LOLIN: And blow the chance to leave this nut house
forever? I'll kill you first.

*(*LILIA *turns away from* LOLIN, *unhappy and torn.)*

LILIA: *(Sad laugh)* He's so afraid I'll get knocked up. I
went on one date all through high school, Lolly. One.
I kissed this guy—and his mouth tasted like salt. Why
does that happen to me? I was holding hands with

him and the next day I have a rash up to my elbow...
why...?

LOLIN: It wasn't Carmelo Alegria's hand...why do you
think?

LILIA: *(Conspiratorially)* Lolly, don't tell Pop, but
sometimes I pretend Carmelo's coming back. This
morning, I found this flower, just growing out of the
wall in my room. I've been making believe he left it for
me...

(LOLIN *looks sadly at* LILIA, *who is absorbed in the flower,
oblivious to everything.)*

LOLIN: Last night I had some date. I made him dinner.
Nice music. New dress. And all night long this sucker's
finding insects crawling in his hair and inside his
ears—bugs! My skin wanted to crawl outta the room
and take a bus to California! And he expected to go to
bed with me! "You can go fuck a can of Raid," I told
him.

(LILIA, *a little shocked, laughs.* LOLIN *puts her arm around*
LILIA. LILIA *is trying to understand her father's position.)*

LILIA: Papi wants grandchildren—he wants to teach his
old stories of Puerto Rico...

LOLIN: *Oye,* I know he's crazy but...deep down...
where there would be a heart if hearts grew inside
rock....I think he's just scared for you. That's why he's
cruising your heart like a patrol cop. Okay? I have to
get my cannibals to school.

(As LILIA *nods her head yes, a small ball of paper comes
sailing over the fence. Soon paper balls fall into the yard like
hail.)*

(LILIA's *twenty-three year old brother,* MILTON, *appears
on the other side of the fence. He's thin, weak, eccentric. His
greasy coveralls say "*MILTON*" on the front and "Tune-up
Masters" on the back.)*

(LILIA *uncrumples a ball and reads.* MILTON *pelts her with paper balls.*)

LILIA: "Dearest Lilia, my wife,
it's me, your predestined husband,
holding in my arms
the children we will never have.
In their eyeless eyes,
I see a reflection of you,
the wife I never married.
Your loving husband, Me."

(LILIA *looks up at* MILTON, *a little confused. He smiles broadly.*)

MILTON: We're gonna be free from the Stalin of Patchogue!

LILIA: Papi's calling you Juan Bobo, Milton, *that's* how pissed off he is—*and* a drug addict.

MILTON: So what? Do I look like I'm scared of him?

LOLIN: Only because he's not here, Macho Comacho.

(MILTON *enters the yard and mockingly makes the sign of the cross over* LILIA. *He intones like* GUZMAN.)

MILTON: "*¡Que Dios te Bendiga!*"

LILIA: Don't make fun of him—

LOLIN: (*Laughs*) I better go. If my kids eat that man's bulldozer, I'll get sued again. Bye-bye, baby. Later.

(LOLIN *kisses* LILIA *on the cheek and exits.* LILIA *looks at* MILTON *sternly.* MILTON *is running around the yard, laughing and dancing.*)

LILIA: Maybe he's right. Maybe you are on drugs.

MILTON: I don't give a damn what he thinks anymore.

LILIA: (*Indicating paper*) And what's this? Who wrote this?

(MILTON *laughs.*)

MILTON: *You know who he is!* He turned eighteen on Monday, same as you! And I've been out, every night this week, trying to pull him to our house with your picture like a magnet—*and I did it!*

(LILIA *looks at* MILTON *with disbelief and anger. He laughs.*)

MILTON: That's right, Carmelo Alegria is back and you two can get married like you're supposed to!

LILIA: Why are—?

MILTON: I don't have to stick around and protect you from Stalin!

LILIA: Why are—?

MILTON: I am free to leave San Quentin and start my life as a cowboy!

LILIA: *Why are you lying to me? (She picks up a poem and rips it.)*

(CARMELO *screams offstage. He appears at the fence.*)

(CARMELO *and* LILIA *stare at each other in disbelief: It's been seven years since they've seen each other.*)

CARMELO: Please be careful with my poems, Lilia, they hurt.

LILIA: *(To* CARMELO*)* That's not Carmelo.

(*Looking at each other, they try to recognize the person they used to know.*)

MILTON: *(Big smile)* Last time you saw each other you were both eleven! And in love, awwww, how cute. But Papi was scared he'd sleep with you. He threw rocks at Carmelo, and chased him out of Patchogue.

LILIA: *(Uncertain)* That's not your face.

CARMELO: Death scratched my face!

MILTON: He traveled all over Latin America. Learned five Indian languages. When he put the skin of those ancient cultures over his bones, he learned their untranslatable secrets.

LILIA: Where's your real face?

CARMELO: It changed the day I saw a resurrection in Mexico City.

MILTON: He saw death everywhere. It followed him around like a dog: poor people, students, travelers, and children who died of hunger and politics and were wiped clean away by flies.

CARMELO: Death's fingernails scratched my face and made me old, Lilia. *(He steps into the yard.)*

*(*MILTON, *drained, lies on the hammock. The bulldozer roars.* LILIA *is wavering.)*

LILIA: Those, those lines on your face are the lines of love. Other girls in other towns.

CARMELO: No, Lilly, every time I looked at another girl, your damn face floated up in front of me and scratched me, deeper than death.

LILIA: *(Smiles)* You smell sweet. Like someone I used to know.

CARMELO: I even thought I saw you coming out of the A-train in New York: I saw a little girl with serious old-woman-eyes and fear smudging her face like candy. I tried to talk to her but her mother hit me on the head with an umbrella!

*(*LILIA *laughs, then catches herself.)*

LILIA: I once had a dream about riding the subway. I dreamed it on Wednesday and Pop says all things dreamed on Wednesday come true.

CARMELO: In all my Wednesday-dreams, I saw a dark room, a candle in the middle of the room, and a Donna Summer record playing over and over again.

LILIA: That was me! I was calling Carmelo...trying to get him back any way I could. *(She looks away.)* The day he left...I fell into bed with a fever...

CARMELO: I *had* to leave. I was a little boy with a grown man's lust in me...

LILIA: *(Smiles)* But Carmelo and I were married when we were eight years old! Mom was our priest. She put on a mustache and she had a bloody nose. She made *pastele* for the reception...

CARMELO: ...and she wrote the marriage license on the back of a telephone bill.

(LILIA looks at him: how could anyone but CARMELO know that?)

CARMELO: It's in your left pocket.

(LILIA, startled, fishes deep in her pocket and finds a folded slip of old paper: their "marriage license." CARMELO recites its contents from memory as LILIA reads silently:)

CARMELO: "By the power vested in me, I, Elena Guzman, pronounce Lilia Guzman and Carmelo Alegria husband and wife."

(LILIA, looking at the license, is fighting tears.)

LILIA: It's the only thing I have in my mother's handwriting. *(Looking at him with final recognition)* She loved you so much, Carmelo Alegria....

(LILIA embraces CARMELO and holds him with all her strength.)

CARMELO: I think promises were made by our parents, before we were born...promises that make us husband and wife.

(The sound of the bulldozer. A special light on MILTON.*)*

MILTON: Last night, I was standing in front of the
Ponderosa House of Western Apparel, staring at a
pair of enchanted cowboy boots. They glowed holy,
beckoning. I dreamed of putting those God-beautiful
boots on my feet and becoming the world's first Puerto
Rican cowboy. I dreamed of moseying over to Stalin
and telling him: I'm going west to change my name
to Clint or Dodge and marry a sunny, white-skinned
cowgirl with high cheekbones and raise li'l ones named
Becky and Roy! *(He laughs, coughs.)* But I'm staring at
those boots, thinking, "Sure Milton, a Puerto Rican
cowboy afraid of horses? Forget it!" That's when I
turned around and saw Carmelo, smiling at me, his
eyes saying, "You don't have to tune cars for a living
anymore. I'm back. I'll take care of your sister. Put
those boots on, get strong, and go west, Milton!" I'm
gonna buy 'em right now!

*(*MILTON *leaps over the fence and exits.* LILIA *and*
CARMELO *hold each other.)*

CARMELO: I know what's going to happen, and our
future isn't going to be very good. We're going to get
old. Our bodies will sputter and slur and stumble for
years before we die. We'll never have money. Our
children will avoid us. In the end, we'll outlive our few
friends and march, tired and blind, to their hundred
funerals.

LILIA: How will we die?

CARMELO: *(Smiles)* Wrapped in each other's old,
wrinkled arms...kissing deep...and getting ready for
one, last death-defying dance in our marriage bed.

*(*LILIA *touches* CARMELO's *hair and mouth, tracing the lines
on his face with her fingertips.)*

LILIA: If these lines are the lines of death, I will put life in them because I love you. *(She kisses him and pulls back.)* Our fathers hate each other and that has to stop. Let's get married and bring our two great families together for all time.

(CARMELO and LILIA kiss. From one of the leafless trees, a big, bright flower blossoms.)

(End of Scene One)

Scene Two

(Later that evening. Cool, slanting lights fill the backyard. The Virgin Mary glows brightly. LILIA is alone.)

LILIA: He took me in his arms, Mom. His muscles lifted me, squeezed tight, and held me higher than the roof of the house—I could see all of Patchogue around me—and he kept pushing me up and up, higher and dizzy—sucking in air—spinning—clouds hitting me on the head—I could touch the warm dome of the sky with my hands, Mom—Mom—*and then he dropped me!* When I fell on the hard bricks of the hammock...my back broke in two. In my coma...all around me...was Carmelo. His voice filling my stomach...his memories squeezing the muscles in my mind...the water of his breath condensing in my lungs and falling in warm drops on my heart. Tonight, when you talk to Papi... will you tell him I sinned?

(We hear footsteps coming from the house.)

GUZMAN: *(Off)* Now stupid! C'mon!

(LILIA, startled, stuffs CARMELO's poems in her pockets and pretends to feed MALINCHE.)

GUZMAN: *(Enters and calls offstage)* Hiberto! Now!

(HIBERTO MUÑOZ *enters. He's a strange, frightened,*
awkward man of thirty-three, with a scraggly beard and a
big ass. He can be played by the actor playing CARMELO.)

HIBERTO: *(Frightened)* She's busy. I'll come back in a
year.

(HIBERTO *starts to exit, but* GUZMAN *stops him, and pushes*
him toward LILIA.)

GUZMAN: Este, Hiberto Muñoz, Lilia Guzman. *(To*
HIBERTO:) What are you waiting for? Move in for the
kill, stupid…

LILIA: No, Papi…no…

HIBERTO: *(Nervous)* I just re-read *Conan the Barbarian,*
which few people appreciate, artwise, despite its
anatomically splendid depiction of bulging muscles
and fat rear-ended women!

LILIA: Mister Muñoz, listen to me…

HIBERTO: *(Panicking)* But why should you care? You're
a beautiful, dark-eyed girl with ripening breasts…and
I'm a hysterical, toad-like substance….

GUZMAN: What are you doing? This is not romance.

(The phone rings.)

LILIA: Pop, something happened today; it changes
everything…

GUZMAN: I'll get that. You young people…stay here…
talk…build a goddamn relationship or I'll break your
heads, *carajo*….

(GUZMAN *exits. Awkward silence.* LILIA *tries to smile.)*

LILIA: I'm sorry, Mister Muñoz, it's not you—

HIBERTO: *You don't have to tell me!* I know! I, I can't
seem to position my body in space. Why is that? Why
is my heart so spastic? My nerves so syncopated?

And I have such needs! Enormous…nuclear-powered needs, Lilia…

(HIBERTO *tries to touch* LILIA*'s breasts—she slaps his hand.*)

LILIA: Mister Muñoz! Please stop! I'm serious!

HIBERTO: Fuck me right now! Fuck me hot and cold!

(HIBERTO *oozes toward* LILIA.)

LILIA: (*Explodes, launching into the unsexiest spiel she can think of:*) My father thinks armed revolution is the only way Puerto Rico will become an independent country.

HIBERTO: Cover me in your hot saliva—lick me 'til I bleed…

(HIBERTO *chases* LILIA *around the yard.*)

LILIA: He calls Puerto Rico a colony of the United States…

HIBERTO: …make me grab my ankles and bark like a dog…

LILIA: …he says the children of Puerto Rico wear Mickey Mouse T-shirts and watch *Bugs Bunny* all day.

HIBERTO: …we'll put mirrors on the ceiling—video machines will capture our gooey climaxes…

LILIA: …Papi's Puerto Rico will have its own heroes on its own stamps…its own art on its own money…and its own vote in the United Nations!

(HIBERTO *has run around so much, his asthma kicks in. He starts wheezing. He sucks on a can of Primatene.*)

HIBERTO: …I want an heir…I want to pass down my genes…

(LILIA *grabs the Primatene.* HIBERTO *pursues her, wheezing, feebly trying to grab the Primatene.*)

LILIA: When Papi was young, he called himself the
Castro of Puerto Rico. But people laughed at him—
even when he collected four hundred charmed
machetes for his army of *jibaros.*

(HIBERTO *is writhing in bronchial agony.)*

LILIA: When Milton turned eighteen, Pop begged him
to lead the revolution. But Milton laughed at him too.
Poor Papi still hopes Milton will take up those rusting
machetes and make a nation.

(LILIA *gives* HIBERTO *the Primatene, which he gratefully
sucks down.)*

HIBERTO: I hope your father doesn't expect me to lead
an army....I'm an asthmatic, a hemophiliac, and a
hypochondriac....

(LILIA *laughs.* HIBERTO *is so pathetic, she feels sorry for him
and impulsively kisses him on the cheek. He sits up.)*

HIBERTO: Wanna kiss the ol' boner? *(Quickly)* Yes, I
know I disgust you. I disgust myself. But I'm thirty-
three years old...and every year some desperate guy
like Guzman throws their virgin daughter at me,
hoping to get rich. But I always say no to them—saving
myself for the best girl, for you.

LILIA: But I'm not the best girl for you. I did something
today. I slept with Carmelo Alegria.

HIBERTO: Oh. What about sloppy seconds—?

(GUZMAN *enters, shaking with rage.)*

GUZMAN: *Those snotty sons-of-bitches in Ponce dug up my
grandmother!* They're saying there's only room in the
cemetery for those who pay! *Dios, por favor: Bring me
the head of Milton Guzman!*

(MILTON *appears, wearing his enchanted boots. The boots
have changed him: He's macho and manly and he looks like*

the Marlboro Man. He brandishes a whip, which he cracks in the air.)

MILTON: Howdyyyyyyyyyyy!!

(GUZMAN looks at him with full contempt. MILTON smiles.)

MILTON: ...call me Juan Bobo once, you old tyrant... and I'll whip the skin off your reptile back, one scale at a time... *(He enters the yard. He swaggers and spits.)*

LILIA: *(Amazed)* You really did it. I don't believe it.

MILTON: I really did it, that's right! *(He picks her up and spins her around. He looks at GUZMAN and HIBERTO ominously.)* And you...you bloated witchdoctor...I ain't takin' your stuff...'cause I am not Milton anymore. I'm Clint—or Dodge—

GUZMAN: The Mafia did it. They turned you into a drug-zombie.

LILIA: No, Pop! His boots are enchanted!

MILTON: Yep! When I put these babies on, lightning danced into my brain and zapped the old me to death on the electric chair. I can see you better than ever: Stalin of Patchogue...Idi Amin of Long Island...

LILIA: *(Worried)* Maybe you should lighten up...

MILTON: *(On a roll)* But that's all bull! Out *there*, where it counts, you're *nobody's* boss, you're a negative, a man without a country. Your birthplace Marcario doesn't even exist! Well, pardner... I am from someplace...and tonight the first Puerto Rican cowboy is going back home—to the Wild American West. *(He cracks the whip.)*

GUZMAN: Do you know what you're doing? You're breaking your mother's heart again. *(Calling to Heaven:)* Isn't that right, Elena?

MILTON: No, uh-uh, you're not going to invoke her...!

GUZMAN: And she's watching her ungrateful son...
aren't you, Elena?

MILTON: Don't bring Mom into this!

(Lights change. On the other side of the fence, the WOMAN
IN THE SHROUD *appears. Over her chest, she's holding a
heart wrapped in flames.)*

MILTON: This is getting to be a weekly thing with you!

GUZMAN: ...and it makes her sick the way you talk to
me and laugh at your heritage...

(The WOMAN *holds up her flaming heart.* MILTON *cracks
his whip.)*

MILTON: *(Pointing to the* WOMAN*)* Does she see you
selling your daughter to Muñoz like a prostitute?!

(Lights change violently. LILIA *hides her eyes.* HIBERTO,
who doesn't see anything, is confused and scared.)

HIBERTO: Maybe I should go...?

MILTON: Mom would never send her to that house of
soulless old men...make her have children she can't
love...

GUZMAN: Lilia's children will be the salvation of this
family!

(Lights get darker. The WOMAN*'s blazing heart glows
brighter.)*

GUZMAN: I've given up waiting for you to produce an
heir.

MILTON: An heir to *what*? An heir to *trash*? To a family,
going back to conquistadors, that lived by killing
Indians, stealing sugar, smuggling rum—! *(He cracks his
whip.)*

*(*HIBERTO, *panicking, pulls out a police whistle and blows
it.)*

HIBERTO: I HAVE TO GO HOME NOW!

(Lights back to normal. The WOMAN *disappears.)*

HIBERTO: Uh…yeah, I'm going home now. *(To* LILIA*:)*
I really love you, Lilia. I waited thirty-three years for
you. I'm sorry you don't love me.

*(*HIBERTO *quickly kisses* LILIA *on the cheek.)*

LILIA: I can't. I'm sorry.

*(*HIBERTO *reaches for her breasts.* LILIA *slaps his hand. He
starts to leave.)*

GUZMAN: Hiberto, son—will you have lunch—?

*(*HIBERTO *exits.)*

GUZMAN: There goes the best man in this goddamn
town. *(He grabs* LILIA *by the shoulders.)* What are you
doing behind my back? Huh?! *Tell me who you love,
coño,* goddammit!

*(*GUZMAN *shakes her roughly. One by one,* CARMELO's
poems fall from the sky.)

*(*LILIA *and* MILTON *try to catch them.* GUZMAN *picks one
up and reads.)*

GUZMAN: "Dearest Lilia, my wife…your loving
husband, Me" *(It takes a moment for the bad news to sink
in.)* You said there was no one.

LILIA: There wasn't—until Carmelo came back.

GUZMAN: For you! Alegria's derelict son is back! And
he wants you! *(Stunned, he stumbles to a bench and sits.)*
Tell me the truth. I won't make a big deal of it. But
you're not a virgin anymore, are you…?

LILIA: We're going to get married—

GUZMAN: *(Laughing bitterly)* ¡Ay, Dios mio! After
everything I've done. All the prayers, fasts, donations
to the church, just to keep this rough world away
from you! *You lied to me! (He motions to slap* LILIA *but he
doesn't. He walks to the chicken coop instead.)* Malinche!

Can you believe this? I broke my back cruising that
toad-like substance Muñoz boy. You got me again,
Alegria!

LILIA: Papi.

GUZMAN: *(To* LILIA*)* You don't know Carmelo's family
like I do. I lived next door to them in Marcario.

LILIA: I know his father. I've been to his house.

GUZMAN: Don't tell me that!

LILIA: He's a lonely old man and he's dying and I help
him because every Wednesday you—*you*—make him
go blind...

GUZMAN: First the father and now the son! *(He looks up
to God.)* I guess a lifetime of doing good wasn't enough
for you!

*(*GUZMAN *spits at the sky—at God—and instantly regrets
it.* LILIA *and* MILTON *cross themselves.)*

*(*GUZMAN *goes to the Virgin Mary and kneels. He turns
on the radio. We hear a simple Puerto Rican folksong and
static.)*

MILTON: Alegria took something from you, didn't he?

*(*GUZMAN *clasps his hands. The music seems to comfort
him.)*

GUZMAN: When I found this statue of the Mother of
God, I was in El Yunque, taking a piss. It was a night
of bright moons and falling stars, the buzz of insects,
the smell of rotting flowers! The Virgin was singing to
me—not from a radio, but with her true voice! I took
her to Marcario and everyone there talked about the
miracle! I was famous overnight! But when I moved to
Long Island and put her in this unholy soil, her singing
turned into dog howling, then A M radio, then static,
then nothing. *(Beat, to statue:)* I need you now....I need

a song to cool the bubbling cesspool in my goddamn mind.

(LILIA *touches* GUZMAN's *shoulder gently.*)

LILIA: I know you don't love Señor Alegria. But please respect my love for his son and give us your blessing.

(GUZMAN *looks at* LILIA, *lost, disoriented. His eyes fill with tears. He struggles to smile.*)

GUZMAN: I don't know Carmelo anymore. Can I keep one of his poems? So I can learn who he is?

(LILIA *gives* GUZMAN *several poems. He puts them in his pocket. He goes to the chicken coop.*)

GUZMAN: I knew this was going to be a strange day. I went to get some eggs this morning. But Malinche's in one of her dirty moods.

(GUZMAN *takes an egg from the chicken coop. It's shaped like a pyramid. He looks at* MILTON *and feebly makes the sign of the cross over him.* GUZMAN *exits.* MILTON *looks at* LILIA *and doubles over laughing.*)

LILIA: Don't laugh at him.

(MILTON *stifles a laugh, smiles, and embraces* LILIA.)

MILTON: I'm leaving tonight. I'm not gonna stop 'til I get to the Texas border. There's gold there. Oil. Babes. (*He kisses her.*) Send me pictures of your wedding, okay?

LILIA: I won't have to. (*She gives him two pictures.*) Me. And Carmelo. Sleep with these pictures under your pillow and you'll see our wedding in your dreams.

(MILTON *takes the pictures.*)

MILTON: You're getting weirder than Pop. (*He laughs and kisses her.*) It's late. The promise of motion is clenching my stomach. I'm not sure, 'cause my Spanish

sucks, but I think *"alegria"* means "happiness."
Goodbye then, Señora Happiness.

LILIA: *Adios*, Clint. Or Dodge.

(MILTON *lets out a long, exulted wolf call and exits. Lights change. End of Scene Two.)*

Scene Three

(Later that night. The Virgin Mary glows with a sick, green light. The radio plays sad music. GUZMAN *enters with* CARMELO's *poem. He looks at the Virgin.)*

GUZMAN: What's wrong with you? Squashing your damn snake and ignoring your friends?! This proves you're dead. I have to go somewhere else. Malinche!

(MALINCHE *runs out of the chicken coop.)*

(MALINCHE *is* GUZMAN's *beloved fighting chicken. Represented by a danger,* MALINCHE *is evil, swift, muscular, and frightening—a true monstrosity.)*

(She runs around, looking for someone to fight. GUZMAN *calms her down by stroking her gently. He folds* CARMELO's *poem into a tight square.)*

GUZMAN: You're the best fighting chicken in the world, *mijita*. Two hundred and nine kills! Now I need you to fight one more time. When I tie this poem to your leg, you're going to make that boy go crazy—and give me your two hundred and tenth kill.

(GUZMAN *makes a backward sign of the cross over the poem. He takes a rubber band from his pocket and reaches for* MALINCHE.)

(A light upstage shoots on, revealing ALEGRIA, CARMELO's *father.* ALEGRIA *is a battered, feeble, nearly blind old man in his sixties. Despite his many ailments, there's great kindness and dignity in old him.)*

ALEGRIA: Don't do it, Guzman, *por Dios*. They're nice kids. They should love each other.

(GUZMAN *stops and looks at* ALEGRIA, *startled.* MALINCHE *lunges at* ALEGRIA. GUZMAN *holds her back.*)

GUZMAN: Alegria! *Que tu haces aqui?* Get out.

ALEGRIA: I'm the one you want, not them. So here I am! Take your last shots! Finish me off! I've already got everything from a tumor in my balls to Lou Gehrig's disease because of your damn spells! (*His laugh shakes his body with pain.*) Oh, and I love the schedule you have me on—

GUZMAN: Get out—

ALEGRIA: —every Monday and Wednesday at two o'clock, I go blind. On Tuesday and Thursday, I'm thrown around the house until I pass out. Have you seen my house? Saturday and Sunday, the roof leaks, rain or shine, and it doesn't leak water, old friend, it leaks piss!

GUZMAN: You mean I forgot Friday?

ALEGRIA: Kill me on Friday, I don't care. Just let our children do what we told God they must do.

(GUZMAN *looks at* ALEGRIA *a beat. He is motionless.* ALEGRIA *hobbles toward him.*)

ALEGRIA: What Elena and I did, *hombre*, that shouldn't affect our children. (*Laughs at the stupidity of it*) Elena and I were kids when we did it! We were bored. It was hot. She didn't even know you then—

GUZMAN: You ruined the girl I wanted to possess since I was old enough to breathe and think!

ALEGRIA: So you're going to hurt Carmelo and break Lilia's heart because of *one night*?

GUZMAN: Because you don't take what belongs to another man! Because my marriage was built on a lie!

Because she married me but she never stopped loving you! Because I deserved someone to love me! I put those spells on you for justice! *I'm sorry you can still walk!*

(GUZMAN *angrily ties the poem to* MALINCHE's *leg.* ALEGRIA *exits.*)

(GUZMAN *and* MALINCHE *dance together.*)

(*The radio cuts off.* GUZMAN *exits. Lights change. End of Scene Three.*)

Scene Four

(*Much later that night. Complete darkness except for a spot on* MALINCHE, *who is alone.*)

(*She completes her wild dance.*)

(CARMELO *appears. He's been awake all night. His eyes are wild and red. His clothes are shreds. He violently mimics the painful gyrations of* MALINCHE's *dance. He screams. End of Scene Four.*)

Scene Five

(*Lights up. The next morning.* CARMELO *is absolutely still. He screams for* LILIA.)

(LILIA *enters. She sees him and starts to say something.*)

CARMELO: No! Be quiet. Don't move—!

LILIA: What happened to you...?

CARMELO: I'm in pain. It's—. (*She tries to step forward.*) *Don't move*—!

LILIA: What is it?

CARMELO: I didn't think I'd make it last night. I didn't think I'd ever see you again—.

(CARMELO *is seized by uncontrollable shaking. He falls into the yard.* LILIA *goes to him. She tries to hold him, but he pushes her away. His body throbs with a force that threatens to pull him apart.*)

CARMELO: It won't let go of me! Tell it to leave me alone!

LILIA: No one's touching you—!

CARMELO: Yes! Tell it to stop! Make it stop! (*He is thrown across the yard. He crashes into the porch. He thrashes about on the floor—then slowly subsides.*) Tell me I'm asleep…tell me it's going to stop….

LILIA: Hold my hand. *Squeeze it as hard as you can.* (*He takes her hand.*) You've got a fever. You're really hot.

CARMELO: I was asleep. Then something grim and stupid picked me up and threw me against the floor like it was trying to break me…

LILIA: I'm taking you to the hospital.

CARMELO: Something like this. Used to attack my dad. But only a few minutes. Not all night—!

GUZMAN: (*Off*) Malinche! Breakfast!

(CARMELO *thrashes violently.*)

LILIA: Papi, I need you! Come over here!

(GUZMAN *enters with chicken feed. The bulldozer roars.*)

CARMELO: It won't let go of me!

LILIA: Carmelo needs help. He's got a fever—

GUZMAN: He's possessed, isn't he…?

LILIA: Forget your fight and help him!

CARMELO: It's burning me!

LILIA: I can't hold him anymore!

GUZMAN: Wait! Don't go anywhere.

(GUZMAN *exits into house.* LILIA *holds* CARMELO *so tightly that his tremors seem to go through her body.*)

CARMELO: God. God. God. God. God.

LILIA: Papi's going to help you. He can cure anything. Once, when I was five, I lost my memory! I forgot how to tie my shoes, or who was Mami, and I kept bumping into walls because I forgot you couldn't walk through them.

(GUZMAN *enters with a bag of pills, a bottle of rum, and a mirror. He goes through a ritual of blessing the objects.*)

LILIA: Then Pop made me drink rum mixed with *malta*, sugar, and one of Malinche's magic eggs. It tasted so bad, it brought my memory back in a second!

(GUZMAN *and* LILIA *take* CARMELO *to the hammock.*)

LILIA: Papi liked your poems. He's going to give us his blessings.

(CARMELO *lies down on the hammock.*)

GUZMAN: This bottle of rum is four hundred years old. My ancestors stole it from Ponce de Leon.

CARMELO: *(Weakly)* Thank you, thank you for helping me....

(GUZMAN *sprinkles rum on* CARMELO. *He screams in pain. He subsides.*)

(GUZMAN *pulls* LILIA *aside.*)

GUZMAN: The soul is so ugly, it can't stand to look at itself. *(He gives her a mirror.)* So hold this in front of his mouth. If he dies, his soul will come out, see itself, get scared, jump back into his body, and keep him alive. *(He goes to* CARMELO.) Take this pill, son. It's a magic drug called Valium.

(CARMELO *swallows the pill.* LILIA *says a Hail Mary.*
GUZMAN *gives* CARMELO *the bottle of rum. He drinks as*
GUZMAN *makes the sign of the cross over him.*)

(CARMELO's *whole body arches in terrible pain.*)

CARMELO: *Help meeeee—Papiiiiii!!!*

(He relaxes. He closes his eyes and lies still.)

LILIA: What's happening? Is he okay?

GUZMAN: *(To* CARMELO*) Como te sientes?*

CARMELO: *(Low)* Cold. Very cold.

LILIA: *(Touching his forehead)* His fever's gone. He's
freezing.

GUZMAN: That's good.

CARMELO: …I feel far away…like I'm miles up in the
air…!

GUZMAN: The rum makes you high…. It's ten thousand
proof.

LILIA: You're going to be okay. What did I tell you?

(CARMELO struggles to open his eyes.)

CARMELO: When I was in Puerto Rico, I went looking
for Marcario…

GUZMAN: *(Low)* Don't talk.

CARMELO: …but I couldn't find it! Then someone told
me…Marcario was ripped up by a hurricane…and
thrown from the world by the Holy Ghost…

GUZMAN: …I don't want you to talk anymore…

LILIA: …do what Papi says….

CARMELO: With your permission! I know you've been
fighting my father…there's bad blood…but I love Lilia.
And I love you. Why can't we forget the past?

(GUZMAN *puts his hand over* CARMELO's *mouth, bidding him to fall asleep, which he does.*)

(LILIA *embraces* GUZMAN. *The bulldozer roars.*)

GUZMAN: Ah. The alarm clock of Patchogue! I better take my tired butt to work, little girl.

LILIA: I love you for helping him!

(LILIA *kisses* GUZMAN. *He pulls away, uncomfortable.*)

LILIA: We're going to have the grandchildren you want! I'm going to tell them your stories and they'll know everything you've ever done.

GUZMAN: Well...I'm not sure what he has...this dumb cure of mine may not work...*tu sabes*, it's all psychology....

LILIA: I know he's going to be okay.

(GUZMAN *kisses* LILIA.)

GUZMAN: Remember, little girl: Sometimes sins are committed...then punishment follows punishment. It's something no one can stop.

LILIA: *(Worried)* What's wrong?

GUZMAN: *(Sadly)* I'm late for work. *(He exits.)*

(LILIA *sits on the hammock next to* CARMELO. *She rocks the hammock back and forth.*)

(GUZMAN *reappears on the other side of the fence. A special light makes him glow. The rest of the stage darkens, slowly.*)

LILIA: Wednesday night, the night you left, I had a dream. It was about two young men living in a forgotten town in Puerto Rico many years ago. They were born on the same day. They cut sugar fifteen hours a day together. Together they dreamed of growing the sweetest sugar in the world and getting rich. They married on the same day. On the same day, their wives became pregnant. Then one of them said to the other: "If your wife has a son and my wife has a daughter—I promise our children will marry each other and bring our families together for all time." Then they shook hands and killed a chicken, dedicating it to the Virgin Mary, and sealing their promise in blood. *(She looks at* CARMELO *and smiles, touching the lines on his face.)* It's finally true, Carmelo. It's finally true.

*(*LILIA *looks at* CARMELO *and kisses him. No response. She kisses him again. No response. She shakes him. She listens for* CARMELO'*s heart, but hears nothing.)*

*(*LILIA *screams—but her scream of panic and pain is eclipsed by the roaring bulldozer.)*

(Lights swiftly change. GUZMAN *lifts his arms.* LILIA *watches, horrified, as* CARMELO'*s soul rises out of his body and disappears.)*

(Lights to black. Final spots on LILIA *and* GUZMAN.*)*

END OF ACT ONE

ACT TWO

Scene One

(A September afternoon. Soft autumn light. The corn stalks are six feet tall. They bulge with big yellow husks.)

(Light on LILIA. She wears a traditional wedding dress and a black armband. She is pale, anorexic. She stands in front of the Virgin Mary, holding a piece of paper and a knife.)

LILIA: Dearest Carmelo, my husband. Milton hasn't written to me.... Mom won't talk to me.... I don't know where else to go. All I do these days is sit by the fence and watch the bulldozers erasing Patchogue. Yesterday, they started dumping chemicals into the pit. So now I stand as close to the rim of the pit as I can. I breathe their heavy air. I fill myself with their waste. I think of my unborn children: how they'll be born deformed, and I won't even care. *(A terrible shudder goes through her body.)* Jesus Christ, what's happening to me?

(Far upstage, a light shows up CARMELO's face. His eyes are closed.)

LILIA: I know what's happening. I'm changing. I will never again feel pride, or pity, or fullness, or great need, ever again. While my soul sings of you, Carmelo, my body falls away, cell by cell, in complete decay. I am now only the invisible bride Hiberto will sleep with tonight...the hollow body where his deformed children

rest before their unhappy birth. (LILIA *folds the paper.*)
Please answer my letter. Your loving wife, me.

(She digs a hole in the ground with the knife. She puts the letter in the ground. She cuts her hand, waters the letter with blood, and covers the letter with dirt.)

(CARMELO disappears.)

(LOLIN enters, wearing a lavender bridesmaid's dress. She's got balloons and streamers.)

(LILIA quickly throws the knife on the ground. LOLIN sees LILIA, gasps—then laughs.)

LOLIN: That's *you!* I'm standing here, going, "Guzman did it: He brought his wife back from the dead!" *(Sniffs)* That's her perfume?

LILIA: *(Weak)* Papi's idea.

LOLIN: You look and smell like the friggin' past. *(Continues putting up balloons and streamers)* It's nice you're wearing your mother's dress. That's respect.

LILIA: It's cold.

LOLIN: You're nervous. I was the same way my first four times. *(Keeping one eye on LILIA, she finishes decorating the yard.)* My kids are in your house, eating. They ate a chair and two plates before I stopped them. So if you want lunch, you better get some fast.

LILIA: I don't want lunch.

LOLIN: Why not?

(No answer. LILIA walks away.)

LOLIN: Do you think I don't watch you? This is like two weeks without food for you, huh?

LILIA: *(Weakly)* What's new with you?

LOLIN: For Chrissakes Lilly, Carmelo is dead, that's all, that's it. He's not in the armband. Or in this heavy air of yours full of poison—

LILIA: Papi said you sold your house…?

(LILIA *walks away from* LOLIN, *trance-like, distant. She stares forlornly into the pit.*)

LOLIN: Yeah. They started dumping some weird new chemical into the pit and Tuesday I caught one of my kids eating a rock that was *glowing*. I said, screw this, I'm getting out of this damn town.

LILIA: Where? Far?

LOLIN: Some place where I can find real men with *spines*…not the…backbones of sugar water and mother's milk holding up the "men" of Patchogue.

LILIA: I hope, when you find your new man, you two will visit me. I hope…in the middle of Muñoz's money…the rooms of our big house…the teeth of our children…I hope you can still find me…. (*She turns away, fighting tears of anger.*)

LOLIN: Lilly, if you don't wanna go through with the wedding, don't. Please. But decide now. A pig's gonna be killed for you—

LILIA: (*Sad laugh*) I decided to marry Mister Muñoz a long time ago. It doesn't bother me.

LOLIN: Hey, maybe he won't be so bad. Huh? He wants you to go to college; he's rich; he's kinda cute. And maybe Carmelo wasn't the—

LILIA: Please don't talk about him.

LOLIN: The truth: Carmelo burned a hole in your heart the size of God, right? And you're ready to fall in that hole and starve to death like…

LILIA: *Dammit, this dress is freezing*—! (*She tears at her wedding dress, ripping pieces from it and throwing them around the yard. She is doing everything she can to fight her tears.*)

(Beat. She calms down, realizing that fighting back is useless.)

LILIA: Sometimes, Lolly, I think I can still hear all the things he ever said to me: all his plans, his ideas. I can see the four children we wanted to have. Do you know where those things went after he died? *(She touches her chest and stomach.)* I do. They're here. I'm saving them inside me. They're waiting for something good to happen in this goddamn world…something truly good…before they come back to be born. *(She looks at* LOLIN, *excited.)* I have to go to the cemetery. Come with me?

LOLIN: Now? The wedding's in an hour—

LILIA: I want to invite him to the wedding.

LOLIN: Lilly! That's bad luck—

LILIA: Don't be afraid. I know a short cut, c'mon.

(LILIA grabs LOLIN's hand and they start to exit. HIBERTO *enters, dressed in a lavender tuxedo. He is an exhausted, nervous wreck.)*

(LILIA and HIBERTO *look at each other—he weakly blows a kiss.)*

HIBERTO: *¡Hola!*

(LILIA and LOLIN exit. In his anxiety and fear, HIBERTO *bursts all the balloons. End of Scene One.)*

Scene Two

(An hour later. HIBERTO *is on the hammock. All the balloons have been popped.)*

(GUZMAN enters, dressed in a big straw hat and baggy suit. He is leading MALINCHE in with a chain. MALINCHE *lunges at* HIBERTO, *who screams.)*

GUZMAN: *¡Hijo!* You missed the killings of the year!
Malinche ripped out eyes and tore stomachs like
she was playing the flute. It was poetry. *(He pulls*
MALINCHE *to her coop and puts her inside. He shows*
HIBERTO *a roll of money. He counts it.)* You're lucky.
Malinche's kills are a good omen. Especially the bloody
ones.

HIBERTO: *(Nervously)* Lucky? I couldn't get out of bed
this morning, ha, ha. Something was holding me down.
It felt like a big hand.

*(*GUZMAN *gives him a look. Before he can respond,* HIBERTO
continues.)

HIBERTO: Then, driving to your house, all four tires on
my brand new Monte Carlo Supreme went flat. *Then I
got lost!* I drove through neighborhoods I've never seen
before. Streets of blood where animals are killed on the
sidewalks and men have tattoos of dead women on
their arms. *(Getting hysterical)* So why did they attack
my car with golf clubs? Why were they trying to keep
me from getting married?

GUZMAN: I've heard of nerves, *pero*, this is fucked up.

HIBERTO: And I'm afraid of Lilia. She changed when
Carmelo died. Her eyes have something in them…
something deep…unforgiving…begging me to fall in
and drown in that blue whirlpool….

GUZMAN: Are you trying to ruin my day or what?

HIBERTO: I'm not in a good enough mood to get
married. I don't think I can touch her tonight—

GUZMAN: You marry her, my friend, and tonight you
touch her. If that means tying her to the bed the way
my great-grandparents did it, *pues*, I'll lend you the
rope myself.

*(*HIBERTO *starts to say something,* GUZMAN *cuts him off.)*

GUZMAN: *Mira,* I want six children. Like Elena and I had. Milton, Lilia, and four who died at birth—four souls killed by the jealous magic of Señor Alegria. They died so fast, some nights I still hear them cry with surprise! *(Puts his arm around* HIBERTO*)* Just make sure you have at least one girl. That way you'll have one who *really* loves you: someone who doesn't go around laughing at you, calling you Stalin. *(He looks at* HIBERTO *very pleased and gives him an affectionate hug as tears fill his eyes.)* You're my son now! That's why I'm giving you the most important thing I have. My book. *(From the inside of the hollowed-out Virgin Mary statue, he produces an ancient, yellowed manuscript.)* "Tales of Marcario." I wrote it for that ungrateful Milton, to teach him the beauty of our culture, and it's all the magic stories that happened in that poor, lost town. *(Opening to the first page)* Page one: "Puerto Rico sits next to the huge U S A—like a little star next to the sun. Poor little country! Getting wiped out by its huge neighbor!" *(Kisses* HIBERTO*)* This book will come in handy when you liberate Puerto Rico for me—.

(Lights change—blackout except for a spot on the back door. Very loud knocking is heard. GUZMAN *goes to the porch.)*

(Lights change wildly. We hear wind—like a hurricane.)

(The back door bursts open and a coffin rolls onto the porch. There's a bill attached to the coffin. A crescendo of noise and lights—then silence. GUZMAN *approaches the coffin, stunned.)*

GUZMAN: *Ay Dios mio, ay Dios.* They really did it.

HIBERTO: What is this? A joke? *This is really funny! Ha! Ha! Ha!*

GUZMAN: Shut up, stupid, it's my grandmother! *(Looking at the bill)* They sent her to me C O D, carajo!!

HIBERTO: Well, what's she doing here?!

GUZMAN: She's rotting!

HIBERTO: Death! Looking at me! Giving me the finger!

GUZMAN: *And people are coming in ten minutes!* Help me get her out of the house before Lolin's kids eat her…

HIBERTO: Oh yes, yes, they're doing it to you, Hiberto…

GUZMAN: *(To house)* …keep away from her, you damn cannibals! *(To* HIBERTO, *who is getting hysterical:)* Don't be so damn supertitious and help me! She's fat, she's got seventy years of flan in her stomach!

HIBERTO: *(Helping drag the coffin into the yard)* I can't do physical work when I'm hysterical! *(He pulls away from the coffin. He desperately goes through the money in his wallet.)* Listen, I'm rich. I can reimburse you for the musicians, pig, rum, everything, just call this off—

GUZMAN: Get a goddamn grip…this doesn't change anything… *(He covers the coffin with streamers.)*

HIBERTO: But she smells like broken promises. And listen, she's making noise. Eating noise. She's digesting herself. *(He throws hundred-dollar bills at* GUZMAN.)* She's dangerous, unlucky and I can't get married in the shadow of this thing!

*(*HIBERTO *starts out again.)*

*(*LOLIN *comes in nearly carrying* LILIA. *They collide with* HIBERTO. LOLIN *is shaking.* LILIA *is deathly pale. She's shivering.)*

LOLIN: Hiberto, Guzman, help me—.

*(*LOLIN, HIBERTO, *and* GUZMAN *carry* LILIA *to the picnic table.* LILIA *sits.)*

GUZMAN: *Que paso?* She's freezing cold!

LOLIN: We were at the cemetery, she fainted. *(To* HIBERTO:)* Get her some water.

*(*HIBERTO *runs into the house.)*

LILIA: I'm cold. This dress is like ice...

(GUZMAN *takes off his jacket and puts it around* LILIA.)

GUZMAN: *(To* LOLIN*)* What were you doing at the cemetery?

(HIBERTO *enters with a glass of water.*)

LOLIN: She invited Carmelo to the wedding.

(HIBERTO *does an about face.*)

GUZMAN: *(To* HIBERTO*)* Get over here with that water!

LOLIN: She put her arms around the tombstone, kissed his name, and passed out.

(HIBERTO *takes the water to* LILIA.)

GUZMAN: *(Concerned)* Talk to me, *hija,* what is it?

(LILIA *stands up and walks away from the table.*)

LILIA: Carmelo's so pretty now! All the dust...the miles...the smells of solitude—all burned from his skin. He's so pure, it hurts to look at him.

(*The radio snaps on, playing party chatter and festive music.* GUZMAN *goes to the fence and looks out.*)

GUZMAN: Ah! The guests are here. The Muñoz family. The Mayor of Patchogue.

(*A car horn tootles "Here comes the bride, all dressed in white."*)

GUZMAN: *(Waves to the guests, then notices)* All their cars have flat tires.

LOLIN: *(To* LILIA*)* If you want to call it off, tell me—

LILIA: No, I'm ready for Hiberto. I'm ready and so is Carmelo.

(*The bulldozer roars. Knocking is heard at the door.* HIBERTO *tries to run out.* GUZMAN *grabs him.*)

GUZMAN: That's the priest. Go keep Lolin's kids from eating him.

LOLIN: If you make her do something she doesn't want, I'll scream bloody murder.

(GUZMAN *pushes* HIBERTO *and* LOLIN *into the house. Party chatter continues.*)

(LILIA *looks at the coffin and smiles.* GUZMAN *looks at* LILIA, *annoyed.*)

LILIA: Look! It's great-grandmother's house!

GUZMAN: Knock it off, put on a better face, and stop this right now—

LILIA: *(Softly)* But maybe it's not a house. Maybe it's a door for me to cross.

GUZMAN: This is disrespectful, sinful, and a big disappointment *para tu mamá*—

LILIA: *(Angry)* Is it? I've been so afraid to face her since she died—but this is her big day—so bring her on—I've got her dress on—I smell like her—*where is she now?*

GUZMAN: Lilia!

(LILIA *looks at* GUZMAN, *frightened. With nowhere else to go, she puts her arms around him, fighting the urge to cry.*)

LILIA: Papi...Papi...nobody knows how he really died....

GUZMAN: Maybe. But let me tell you, your sweet boyfriend wasn't so innocent. They said he died of drugs—.

(LILIA *pulls away.*)

LILIA: Really? Well, let me tell you, Pop, some people don't believe that story.

GUZMAN: *(Angry)* What do they believe? *(No answer)* Huh? *What do they believe?*

(LILIA *walks from* GUZMAN *to the fence and looks at the pit.*)

LILIA: Don't worry. I'll put on the face you want. I'll make you proud of my lies.

(LILIA *gives back* GUZMAN'*s jacket. He puts it on. She puts on a smiling mask.*)

(The PRIEST *enters. Played by the actor playing* ALEGRIA, *the* PRIEST *wears traditional clerical robes, a big mustache, and a bloody nose.* HIBERTO *and* LOLIN *enter. They carry cardboard cutouts of people—these are the wedding guests. The radio plays happy party music.)*

GUZMAN: *Padre, Padre, Padre,* I'm so glad you made it.

PRIEST: Am I really here? Should I be somewhere else? Will the people in that other place miss me if I'm not there?

GUZMAN: Uh, no—

PRIEST: You're lucky you're not me. Your clerical collar would have snapped out of your shirt, whacking you on the nose, blood all over the place, you arrive, your nose unclogs, then dead air assaults your nose from— *What the fuck is that coffin doing here!?*

GUZMAN: *(Panicking)* I—I was very close to my *abuelita*—I didn't want her to miss this.

LOLIN: *(To* GUZMAN*)* She shouldn't get married, *bruto,* she still loves Carmelo.

(GUZMAN, *desperate to get this over with, stands on the porch and faces the crowd.*)

GUZMAN: Mister and Mrs Muñoz, shareholders of Muñoz Inc., welcome! ¡*Bienvenidos!* Today you're going to see the fabulous marriage of my little girl to this upwardly mobile young Hiberto. You're going to see the slaughter of a big expensive pig! And nine months from tonight, if Hiberto does his job right…

(Canned laughter from radio)

GUZMAN: ...the dreams and sorrows of our people will pass on to a new generation. *¡Que Dios te bendiga!*

([Applause. Party chatter.] GUZMAN *pulls* LILIA *aside, straightens out her dress and veil, gives her a bouquet, and kisses her.)*

GUZMAN: *Oyeme,* Lilia, your mother just arrived! She always liked to make a big entrance! See? She's watching you. She's wearing the tinsel earrings you gave her on Mother's Day—. *(Getting choked up)* Hold on to your mother, Lilia; hold, hold for strength.

(Lights change. The radio plays the traditional wedding march.)

*(*HIBERTO, *shaking, takes* LILIA's *arm.* GUZMAN *signals them to start the march up the aisle. They stand in front of the* PRIEST.*)*

(The PRIEST *starts frantically flipping through the pages of the Bible. He is beginning to panic.)*

GUZMAN: What's the problem, *Padre?*

PRIEST: Uh. Am I confused? Is this a wedding? Is this the Bible? All these words are wrong—

GUZMAN: Read them anyway; they're only words.

LILIA: Read them, please! They're beautiful words... *(She takes off her smiling mask and holds it over her head. The look on her face is the look of ecstasy.)*

PRIEST: *(Reading)* "Dearest Lilia, my wife..."

LILIA: *(Gasps)* Oh! Your hand is warm!

PRIEST: *(Reading)* "...I look at my left hand and see the ghost of the wedding ring you never gave me—."

GUZMAN: Whoa, whoa, *what are you doing? (He grabs the Bible from the* PRIEST *and flips through it.)* "Dearest Lilia, my wife..." "Dearest Lilia, my wife..." Every damn page? What is this?

(LILIA's *body is going through a transformation as* CARMELO's *soul enters her. She speaks in a low whisper, like a prayer.*)

LILIA: ...yes, my love, yes, my dearest...

GUZMAN: *(To* PRIEST*)* Do I have to do everything myself?

(GUZMAN *rips the bloody collar from the* PRIEST. *He pushes the* PRIEST *out of the way and throws the Bible into the pit. Everyone gasps.*)

(GUZMAN *holds the collar in the air and faces the young couple.* HIBERTO's *asthma kicks in.*)

GUZMAN: By the power vested in me by my great-grandfather who played dominoes with Saint Thomas Aquinas...

LILIA: I'm ready...

GUZMAN: ...by *tia* Julia who was hit by lightning on Good Friday and can tell the future by counting the hairs in your ears...

LILIA: ...take me with you...

GUZMAN: ...I, Pedro Guzman, pronounce Lilia Guzman and Hiberto Muñoz husband and wife! What I have brought together let no man tear asunder!

LILIA: ...take me with you...

GUZMAN: *(To* HIBERTO*) You may now kiss the bride!*

(HIBERTO *tries to kiss* LILIA.)

(*Lights change.* LILIA *pushes* HIBERTO *away with incredible strength.*)

(*She throws her mask to the ground and smashes it with her foot.*)

(LILIA's *possession is wild, violent, frightening. Her body goes out of control, writhing, spinning, and shaking with supernatural energy.)*

LILIA: (CARMELO) Noooooooo! Leave my wife alone! I'm not going to let you kiss my wife!

(All look at LILIA, *stunned by the terrible and beautiful transformation.)*

GUZMAN: *What are you doing? ¡Pale un beso!*

LILIA: (CARMELO) I'm not going to let you give my wife away! You can't do that—!

*(*GUZMAN *tries to grab* LILIA.*)*

GUZMAN: Lilia, stop—people are looking at you...

*(*LILIA's *movements reach a climax—then stop.)*

LILIA: (CARMELO) I am not Lilia. I am your best friend's son. I am Carmelo Alegria.

(From the radio we hear the howling of dogs. The bulldozer screams.)

(The flower, which blossomed at the end of ACT ONE, Scene One, dies and falls from the tree. A rain of black flowers falls from the sky.)

(People scream, trying to get out of the way of the flowers. During this storm, LILIA *is completely still.)*

*(*LILIA *faints. All freeze.)*

(A spotlight reveals MILTON, *far away in Texas. He suddenly, violently wakes up, as if being jolted from a nightmare.)*

MILTON: *LILIA!*

*(*MILTON *reaches under his pillow and takes out the pictures of* CARMELO *and* LILIA. *He looks at them. Lights down on* MILTON. *End of Scene Two)*

Scene Three

(Lights change in the yard. The guests look at the prostrate
LILIA.*)*

GUZMAN: *(Low, ashamed)* Everybody out. Get out of my
backyard.

*(*GUZMAN *carries* LILIA *to the hammock.* LOLIN *and*
HIBERTO *remove the cardboard people.* LOLIN, *the* PRIEST,
HIBERTO, *and* GUZMAN *exit.)*

*(*LILIA *is alone, asleep.)*

*(Lights come down—we go from high afternoon, to evening,
to late night. There's moonlight and silence.)*

(Upstage, lights on MILTON. *He's dressed in cliché cowboy
clothes with toy six-shooters in holsters.* MILTON *practices
his quick draw.)*

MILTON: Howdy. I'm Clint, or Dodge, and I'm here to
tell you, Lilia, it's beautiful out west. I feel like I was
created out here…like I'm a sibling of the cactus…
daddy to the wide, flat, moonland of Arizona. *(Practices
his quick draw)* I got proof for Stalin that good stories
can happen in the U S A. In a Texas town there was a
woman who stole children from their cribs and sold
them as slaves to coyotes and wolves. Well pardner,
the outraged parents of those kids got together and
hired a medicine man, to kill the witch for a small fee.
Well, it took a while, but when they gave him those
glistening piles of gold and buckets of jewels…he ran
to the woman's house and turned her into a cow. Then
those awe-struck parents descended on that cow—and
tore her apart with their teeth. Yes, Lilia, they chewed
her to death and tossed her stick-bones to the dawgies.

(Light around MILTON *changes.)*

MILTON: That's the news from here. I'm having weird
dreams about you, Lilia; hope they ain't true. *(Nervous*

laugh) As for me, well ma'am, I'm gonna keep on going as long as my luck...my luck...my luck...holds out....

(MILTON shoots the audience. He pantomimes being shot and killed. Lights down on Texas.)

(GUZMAN enters from the house, a little drunk, a bottle of rum in one hand and a plastic garbage bag in the other. He puts flowers, streamers, and other wedding debris into the bag.)

(Offstage we hear his telephone ringing.)

GUZMAN: *(Softly)* You should hear the gossip. Hiberto is telling everybody the worms in my grandma's coffin took away his bride. Our phone won't stop ringing. Even after I unplugged it. *(Laughs)* Fullano Torres wants you to touch his son's face so your "miracle" will take away his zits! *(Laughs, picks up litter)* For the first time ever, people in this ignorant town want to hear stories about Marcario! *(He drinks sadly.)* Hiberto's gone. *Se fue.* Took his money with him. I have to go back to Lockheed and grind my fingers to pulp, Lilia, *thanks a lot. (He picks up more litter.) Nooooo!!* I didn't believe, for one second, it was Carmelo coming back from the dead. Resurrections don't happen in this damn, empty U S A! *So get up!*

(Phone stops ringing.)

GUZMAN: I want to tell you about Luis Santana, a nice boy whose father owns a Mobil station in Ronkonkoma.

(LILIA laughs. GUZMAN laughs nervously.)

LILIA: *(CARMELO)* Lilia can't talk. She's in shock. There's not much room in the human body—two souls get a little crowded in here—

GUZMAN: There's no one here; you can stop now; and okay, *don't* get married—

LILIA: (CARMELO) I shouldn't have come. This could hurt her. But she called me—there was electricity—a freefall—she said "Let's live together, live in sin".

GUZMAN: (Getting angry) Goddammit, all you're doing is acting like a scared *mocosa* too damn selfish to give me grandchil—

LILIA: (CARMELO) —and I said yes! Now I'm home! After all my travel, my trouble, I'm someplace that wants me, Guzman.

GUZMAN: *I'm not Guzman—I am Pa-pi!! (He drunkenly takes off his belt.)*

LILIA: (CARMELO) Yes! The belt! Still the bully you always were—.

(GUZMAN *whips the coffin with his belt.)*

GUZMAN: Papi! Papi! Papi!

(At the sound of the whipping, LILIA *stands. She points at* GUZMAN. *He stops.)*

LILIA: If you touch my dear wife with that belt, hurt her in any way…I'll come into your sleep tonight…I'll walk into your wildest dreams…and I'll pull your goddamn mind *apart. (Beat)* As sure as you killed me with poison, I can kill you with fear.

(GUZMAN *looks at* LILIA, *truly frightened. He puts his belt on, shaking.)*

GUZMAN: You're really on a roll, aren't you? I didn't kill anybody.

LILIA: (CARMELO) As I twisted free of my ruined body, I saw your acts of contrition, holding Lilia's hand at the funeral, then walking her to the cesspool-bed of Hiberto Muñoz. If I were alive, I would have thrown up!

GUZMAN: (Shaken) …That's enough, Lilia…let's eat dinner and watch a little T V….

(LILIA *lets out a sad laugh that freezes* GUZMAN.)

LILIA: (CARMELO) I know everything now! That's right!
I know Elena doesn't talk to you! That's a lie you made
up to keep Lilia in line. I know the dead are nothing
but spectators, Guzman.

GUZMAN: (*Frightened*) What? Angels.

LILIA: (CARMELO) No, not angels. The dead don't fly.
They don't move at all. The dead sit in a big, dark
movie theater in outer space, Guzman, in stiff wooden
chairs a million miles apart: eyes front, backs straight,
mouths shut. On the screen they watch forever is the
movie of all the lives of all people in the world. That
doesn't sound so bad, does it? The problem is, when
you die, you take all your emotions with you. So when
your wife marries a man she loves more than you,
and your house decays, and your kids self-destruct…
you go through all the pain you thought you left
behind when you died. It's hell! All those lonely souls
watching new wars begin, famines blossoming in the
desert, and the amazing stupidity of nations. Some
night soon…when the TV is off…turn your ear to the
stars and you'll hear these souls cry like children.

(GUZMAN *hurls his bottle at the fence, smashing it.*)

GUZMAN: *You're lying!* When I die, I'll be damned if
I turn into a zombie watching movies in space. I've
confessed too many crimes and paid the devil too
much insurance! I will get the death I've been working
for!

(LILIA *laughs, shaking her head in amazement. She sits on
the coffin.*)

LILIA: (CARMELO) This death is no better than you
deserve, Guzman! Remember, I know everything! I
know some pretty good family history! (*Beat*) I know
my father slept with your wife before you did. I know

Elena was afraid you'd kill her if you found out she
wasn't a virgin on your wedding night. I know she
tricked you: She got you so drunk that night, you
couldn't even touch her, and the next morning, she
said you had taken her virginity—

GUZMAN: Who told you this…?

LILIA: (CARMELO) And I know you punished her for
this! You created a myth! The myth of the perfect
marriage. You made everyone believe she was happy.
That you loved her. But deep in this pit, where no one
could stop you, she was a prisoner to your sarcasm,
your ridicule, your jealousy, your endless fooling
around. I know she was so unhappy *she finally starved
herself to death*—

GUZMAN: *Who told you all this?!*

(GUZMAN *rushes at* LILIA *and shakes her roughly.*)

(LOLIN *appears at the top of the fence with a plate of food.*
GUZMAN *lets* LILIA *go.*)

LOLIN: Remember the pig you were going to kill? It
escaped. Ran to Macy's and took the elevator to the
fifth floor, where the bridal shops are, and the animal
went berserk. It ate wedding dresses. It swallowed
diamond rings. It trampled crystal, toasters, wine
glasses, and silk pajamas. When they finally shot it, it
was wallowing in the remains of a chocolate wedding
cake. The devastation is so complete, there won't be
another wedding in Patchogue for seven years.

(LILIA *lies on the hammock.* GUZMAN *looks at her, drained.
The phone rings. He staggers toward the house.*)

GUZMAN: Why is she doing this to me? I've been a
perfect father.

(GUZMAN *exits.* LOLIN *goes to* LILIA. *She puts the steaming
plate of food under* LILIA*'s nose.*)

(The offstage phone stops ringing. LILIA *stirs, yawns, and smiles weakly.* LOLIN *sighs with relief.)*

LOLIN: Lilia?

LILIA: Lolly…? What do I smell? Heaven?

LOLIN: Close. It's my sausage and yellow rice…

LILIA: Oh…

LOLIN: …black beans and *tostones* to commit serial murder for…

LILIA: …Oh…!

LOLIN: …which you have to eat because I made a ton for someone's wedding and then she crapped out on me.

LILIA: *(Laughs)* I'm not hungry, Lolly—*he's* with me. *(Laughs)* He thinks he's hurting me!

LOLIN: He is! You're burning with a fever I feel from here!

LILIA: I don't care if I die—

LOLIN: If you don't eat, I'm gonna drag you to a hospital and stick a tube of food in your arms.

*(*LILIA *laughs. She reaches up to* LOLIN *and kisses her.)*

LILIA: I have him now. Just when I thought I'd never touch him again. I'm going to enjoy every second of him…enjoy him filling me like the ocean poured into a cup. *(Beat)* I'm selfish now. When I die, will you make sure Pop buries me next to my husband?

*(*LILIA *passes out.* GUZMAN *staggers out of the house, a big smile on his face. He's holding a cordless telephone.)*

LOLIN: *(To* GUZMAN*)* What are you so happy about?

(From the sky, a movie marquee comes down over the yard, saying "Touch the Miracle. Ten Dollars." The Christmas lights around the sign are festive and cheap.)

GUZMAN: *(Laughing)* Hiberto called the T V stations! They're sending a film crew to my house to see Lilia! It's on the news! We're going to be famous!

(Lights up. GUZMAN goes back into the house. End of Scene Three.)

Scene Four

(LOLIN is looking at the flashing sign. She smiles.)

LOLIN: Famous?

(Lights change to highlight LOLIN. The marquee stops flashing. LOLIN speaks to the audience.)

LOLIN: I had another date last night. After dinner we're on the sofa. The boys are in their rooms. And my date begins exploring my unchartered terrain. Colonizing me. Putting down resistance. Putting up the flag of his superpower. I close my eyes, ready for the nuclear attack that will rip me with shrapnel and spit....

(A white flash of light. LOLIN laughs.)

LOLIN: Then I hear laughing! It's my boys! They're in the living room taking polaroids of Mommy about to go down on her date. And so help me, it strikes me as the funniest thing they've ever done. I start laughing. My boys are laughing. Then I notice my date's not laughing. He's adjusting his zipper, looking grim, and I ask him where his sense of humor is and he puts on a pair of brass knuckles that give his fist the density of a tank and he punches my oldest son in the face, sending his teeth all over the room. I start screaming. My son is unconscious. My other sons are trying to set my date on fire with kitchen matches and my oldest boy, my sweetheart, my love, is now in a hospital, swimming up to stable condition. For Chrissakes, I'm thirty-nine years old. I can't take another date like this.

ACT TWO   55

*(Lights change. The marquee continues flashing. It's now
several days later. Bright autumn afternoon)*

*(LOLIN stands by the door, waiting to pounce on GUZMAN.
LILIA is lying motionless on the hammock.)*

*(GUZMAN enters, wearing a tuxedo. The bandages around
his fingers are gone. He wears big, expensive rings and gold
chains. He separates LILIA from the rest of the yard with red
velvet cord. He covers her with rosaries and crucifixes.)*

*(GUZMAN talks into the cordless telephone, making deals
with a Hollywood agent.)*

GUZMAN: Love it…beautiful…fabulous…epic!

(GUZMAN sees LOLIN. She smiles.)

LOLIN: Guzman. *(Beat)* Yo, Guzman.

*(MILTON appears. His cowboy clothes are dusty and torn.
His magic boots are worn almost to nothing. He still has his
whip. He watches the following angrily:)*

(LOLIN crosses to GUZMAN.)

LOLIN: I need a winner in my life. A man who's been
on the cover of a magazine.

*(LOLIN crosses to the porch, beckoning GUZMAN to follow
her inside. He talks into the phone.)*

GUZMAN: Catch you later, babe. You're a knucklehead.

*(GUZMAN puts the phone away, smiles lustily, and follows
LOLIN.)*

*(MILTON enters the yard and cracks his whip. The flashing
marquee stops flashing. The sound of the whip freezes
GUZMAN in his tracks. GUZMAN forces a smile.)*

GUZMAN: *Pues, mira que cosa,* I knew my son would
come back when he heard his old pappy was lookin'
good. Like the tux?

MILTON: Uh-huh, you're pimped out nice and fine,
Pop.

GUZMAN: Did you hear? I quit my job at Lockheed. Goya Foods wants me to endorse their new line of beans. I'm on the cover of six magazines—

MILTON: I was crawling over Texas on my belly, Pop, dust boulders in my eyes, and the sun playing soccer with my senses—

GUZMAN: *(Holding up phone)* Milton, that was the *coast...*

MILTON: —and when I got to a bar in Corpus Christi that had goddamn Nixon portraits done in velvet on the walls, I heard a man singing a ballad called, "I Thought You Was Dead Carmelo, 'Til You Crashed the Party in My Soul, *Baby."*

GUZMAN: They want to make a movie!

MILTON: When was the last time she ate? Huh?

GUZMAN: And look—my fingers—they haven't seen sunlight since 1968—

MILTON: The radio says she's in a coma, but as the profits pile up, you won't let her see a doctor—

GUZMAN: And the best part is, Milton, if they make this movie, a story about *our people* will be famous—

MILTON: Lilia, can you hear me?

GUZMAN: —and for once, our story isn't about muggers and hookers and heroin addicts; it's about *amor*, real love—

MILTON: But I can feel her fever *two feet away*—!

(MILTON takes GUZMAN's hand and puts it on LILIA's forehead, which burns GUZMAN's hand like a hot stove. He pulls his hand away and blows on his burnt fingers.)

GUZMAN: I've been waiting for this all my life, Juan Bobo! The governor of Puerto Rico is sending out an

expedition to find Marcario! This story could start a
revolution that—!

MILTON: She's not going to be a martyr for your
doomed, half-assed revolution—

GUZMAN: She's not going to die! *(He whispers so* LOLIN
can't hear.) I know this looks bad, but Carmelo didn't
come back from the dead; Lilia is pretending.

MILTON: *She's pretending a fever—?*

LOLIN: *(Impatient)* Guzman! Listen! That's the iron
jacket around my heart unzipping itself for you...

*(*LOLIN *enters the doorway.* GUZMAN *quickly follows. They
embrace and go through an erotic and beautiful pose before
exiting into the house.)*

*(*MILTON *turns away in disgust. He goes to* LILIA. *He tries
to make her eat a candy bar. She won't. He shakes her.)*

MILTON: Lilia, listen, it's Milton.

LILIA: *(Very weakly)* ...Milton...?...Oh...how are you...?

MILTON: Sucko. The West was a bummer. *(No response)*
I got all excited when I heard about a woman who was
turned into a cow and eaten by her neighbors. But it
wasn't true. Turns out they were shooting a movie
about a woman who was turned into a cow and eaten
by her neighbors.

LILIA: ...I'm sorry...it's hard for me to talk...

MILTON: Come on! You remember who else starved
herself? Mom did! Remember we had to jump her and
try to make her eat crackers and she wouldn't and we
cried all night?

LILIA: ...don't be hard on Papi...I refused the
exorcism...

MILTON: What about us? What happens to us when
you die?

(No response. MILTON tries to lift LILIA—but she's so hot, she burns his hands. He puts her down and pulls away, blowing on his hands.)

(LILIA suddenly stands up. She points at the chicken coop.)

LILIA: *(CARMELO)* Milton…go look…at Malinche…go look at Malinche….

(MILTON goes to the coop and opens the door. MALINCHE leaps out. MILTON pulls CARMELO's poem from MALINCHE's leg. He unfolds it and reads.)

(MILTON rips the poem. MALINCHE lunges at him, clawing him viciously. He throws MALINCHE off and reaches for his whip.)

(It's a fight to the death. MILTON whips her as she tries to claw him. A weird, ear-splitting scream fills the theater each time he hits her.)

(MILTON mercilessly whips MALINCHE until her unbearable screams die down and her deformed soul leaves her body.)

(GUZMAN runs into the yard, buttoning his shirt. He looks at the dead MALINCHE. MILTON grabs GUZMAN.)

MILTON: Half of me wants to call the cops on you, Pop. Only how do I tell them your accomplice in Carmelo's murder was a goddamn chicken?! *(He twists GUZMAN's arm behind his back.)* Now don't expect me to believe Lilia's safe with you—

GUZMAN: I wouldn't hurt her. I love her—

MILTON: You love her?! You only love what you *diminish*, you goddamn Stalin! *(He pushes GUZMAN to the coffin and opens the coffin door.)* Why don't you let your half-dead daughter teach you what love is? She really does love you; she's pure for you. But like the Mafia destroying the woods in Patchogue, you have to ruin that purity every chance you get! Well, she's not going to die so you can sell Goya Beans!

(MILTON starts pushing GUZMAN into the coffin.)

GUZMAN: I've been poor all my life! Let me enjoy myself this one time!

MILTON: Not until you see where you're sending my sister!

(MILTON pushes GUZMAN in the coffin and slams the door lid behind him. GUZMAN pounds on the door from the inside.)

GUZMAN: You're a scumbag! Open this door!

(The back door opens and ALEGRIA enters. He is older, weaker, and shabbier than before. He is held up only by his cane and willpower.)

(As GUZMAN pounds and screams, ALEGRIA walks to LILIA, looks at her sadly, and kisses her. The pounding grows more frantic. ALEGRIA smiles weakly.)

ALEGRIA: That's a sound I've been waiting to hear for a long time, Milton. Pedro Guzman languishing in hell.

(ALEGRIA laughs weakly, coughs. End of Scene Four.)

Scene Five

(Continuous action. ALEGRIA is looking at LILIA. GUZMAN's knocking and entreaties are weaker.)

GUZMAN: ...Okay, you're not a scumbag...please... grandmother's got her hands all over me...her fingers are in my throat...*I don't want to see what I see in here...!*

(GUZMAN starts to cry. MILTON can't stand it and opens the coffin door.)

(GUZMAN comes out. His clothes are torn to shreds. MILTON wipes cobwebs and corpse debris from GUZMAN's clothes. GUZMAN is shivering. He doesn't yet see ALEGRIA.)

GUZMAN: Milton, I saw it...the whole thing, like Carmelo said....

MILTON: Take it easy. You're gonna live.

GUZMAN: ...There's a movie theater out there...dead people watching us...crying....*I saw your mother and she's mad at me for doing this*....I can't let Lilia die, Milton....

ALEGRIA: You better hurry.

(GUZMAN *turns around, startled. The two old adversaries look at each other a moment.* GUZMAN *smiles with hope.*)

GUZMAN: Alegria...?

ALEGRIA: The two souls in Lilia's body are making love. The heat of that love is killing your little girl.

GUZMAN: You're here to help her, aren't you? Thank God—!

ALEGRIA: I'm here because I heard on the news that my son was making a comeback and I wanted to say hello.

GUZMAN: But you can tell Carmelo to leave her. Carmelo respects you! He'll listen to his father!

(ALEGRIA *turns away from* GUZMAN.)

GUZMAN: She was good to you. She brought you food and read to you when you went blind—she made you laugh—and I encouraged her!

ALEGRIA: I'm prepared to let her die, Guzman, because her death is the one death that would really break you....

GUZMAN: Please help her, Alegria, please, please, I'll do anything.

(ALEGRIA *looks at* LILIA *and holds her hand. He shakes his head sadly.*)

ALEGRIA: Two people dead. One crippled. One about to die. And predestined children left unborn. For what?

For pride? For a little gold to decorate the hallways of your old age?

GUZMAN: ...*Bendito, bendito*....

(LILIA *moans in pain.* GUZMAN *goes to her, trembling.* ALEGRIA *looks at her sadly.)*

ALEGRIA: My poor Carmelo. Calling to us from this beautiful graveyard and begging us for the wife we promised him.

(LILIA *screams. Her pain goes through* ALEGRIA.)

ALEGRIA: No, no, no, goddammit, it's not fair to visit our stupid war on our children. I will talk to Carmelo—I will make him leave—but it's going to cost you, Guzman.

GUZMAN: Anything. I don't care what.

ALEGRIA: You have to give me something you love.

GUZMAN: Take Milton—

ALEGRIA: I want your watch. The one that goes backwards.

(GUZMAN *looks at him, stunned. Beat)*

GUZMAN: What are you going to do with it?

ALEGRIA: We were born on the same day, you and me. But while I'm dying of old age, you don't have a grey hair on your head and I don't think that's fair.

GUZMAN: *Bueno,* I take care of myself—

ALEGRIA: So listen to me. When you give me your watch, you're going to give up the power inside it—the power that keeps you young.

(GUZMAN *looks at* ALEGRIA *in disbelief.)*

ALEGRIA: You're going to give up the Virgin Mary, and the magic corn, and all your knowledge of magic: the knowledge that ruined my health, blasted my hopes, and killed my son.

GUZMAN: *(Backing away)* That's everything I have.

MILTON: Give him the goddamn watch, Pop.

(MILTON goes to GUZMAN and rips the watch from GUZMAN's pocket. MILTON gives the watch to ALEGRIA.)

(ALEGRIA goes to LILIA.)

ALEGRIA: Carmelo. It's your old man calling. We have to talk.

(Lights down to near black. End of Scene Five.)

Scene Six

(Continuous action. In the dark, downstage, ALEGRIA traces a circle on the ground with his cane, which slowly fills with pulsating light.)

ALEGRIA: This is a magic circle, son. As long as you stay inside it, nothing will hurt you.

LILIA: *(CARMELO)* "Dearest Lilia, my wife…

CARMELO & LILIA:
…we have been dead a hundred years.
Our bones are dust
And our dry memories have disappeared…

CARMELO: …your loving husband, Me…."

(CARMELO appears. He's in a white suit, looking young and handsome.)

(He walks to LILIA. Suddenly she is the healthy, happy teenager we saw in the beginning. She and CARMELO embrace and kiss.)

(Laughing, they walk into the magic circle. For a while, they can look only at each other. Nothing else exists.)

ALEGRIA: *(To* LILIA*)* How do you feel?

LILIA: Hot…a little hungry… *(Quickly)* …but that doesn't matter because I have your son with me. I have everything I need.

ALEGRIA: *Y tu también,* Carmelito? Do you have everything you need?

CARMELO: *(Unsure) Sí,* Papi, I do.

ALEGRIA: You sound a little guilty, son…are you okay—?

LILIA: *(Quickly)* Everything's fine. We have everything figured out. Right Carmelo?

CARMELO: *(Hesitant)* We're going to have children, Papi. The grandchildren you always wanted.

LILIA: Two girls and two boys. Pedro, Elena, Carmelo, and Teresa, named after their grandparents.

(Beat. ALEGRIA *looks at them sadly.)*

CARMELO: What's the matter? You know Lilia and I are married….

*(*ALEGRIA *goes to the hammock and picks up the crucifixes that had been covering* LILIA.*)*

LILIA: Don't we have your blessings?

*(*ALEGRIA *starts placing crucifixes around the edge of the magic circle.)*

ALEGRIA: Lilia, for Godsakes, you're alive! And poor Carmelo's just air! How can you have children?

LILIA: It's—it's—

ALEGRIA: I raised you to be honest, Carmelo—be honest with me.

CARMELO: I know they'll never be born. It's just something we talk about….

ALEGRIA: If they can never be born, Carmelo, why are you still here?

LILIA: It was my idea! I brought him here!

ALEGRIA: Are you a coward, son? Can't you face death alone?

CARMELO: I'm not a coward, Papi...

ALEGRIA: Or don't you want her to live a good long life...?

CARMELO: ...Of course I do....

LILIA: No! If you can't live, Carmelo, I don't want to...

ALEGRIA: I know what's keeping you from leaving! You're jealous and afraid. You don't want her to meet a man she can love in *this* world—

LILIA: All I want is my life with Carmelo—

ALEGRIA: What life? Lying on that hammock, delirious, thirsty, in pain—that isn't life.

LILIA: Life on that hammock was deeper and sweeter than any I ever had—

ALEGRIA: (*To* CARMELO) Are you really going to send her to that movie theater—before she's even ready?

CARMELO: Papi—

ALEGRIA: You died before your time son, I miss you too, I want you back...but you've had time to think about your death and be with your wife. (*He puts down the last crucifix.*) Now...*you must go before you kill her.*

(CARMELO *turns away from* LILIA *for the first time. She looks at him, frightened.*)

LILIA: What's wrong?

(*It takes* CARMELO *a moment to respond. He can't look at* LILIA.)

CARMELO: I've been trying not to hear your screams or feel your fever.

LILIA: What are you saying?

ALEGRIA: Say it, son. Make me proud of you.

CARMELO: Papi's right. We've been fooling ourselves. We're in two different worlds—

LILIA: I'll go with you—

CARMELO: I don't want you to die—your life is too dear to me—

LILIA: Yours was dear to me but I gave you nothing while you were alive. This is the one thing I thought I could give.

CARMELO: But we can't be together when you die, we'll—

LILIA: But we're together *now.*

CARMELO: What's now? Only hours.

LILIA: *So let me have those hours!*

CARMELO: I have to go—

LILIA: Do you know how you're asking me to live? Every place and hour and thing in this world will be empty of you—and I don't want a world like that....

(The lights around CARMELO *change slightly.)*

LILIA: What was that? What do I feel? *(No answer) I want to know what that was!*

CARMELO: —it's not your time to go...it's not your time....

ALEGRIA: Now son. Now.

LILIA: I saw them bury you—I cried for you like no wife ever cried for her husband—please, *I can't stand to see you die again—*

ALEGRIA: *(Overlapping)* ...Dear God, accept the soul of my son, Carmelo Alegria....Hold him in your infinite hands and protect him, shower him with mercy and let him rest...

(GUZMAN and MILTON kneel down in prayer, repeating ALEGRIA's invocation.)

CARMELO: *(Overlapping)* They're pulling me and they're strong—

LILIA: I'm strong too! *You can hold on to me—!*

CARMELO: I can't...I can't...I'm sorry...

(The magic circle brightens. LILIA screams.)

CARMELO: ...it's time.

LILIA: *(Screams)* No. Noooooooooooooooo! Carmelooooooo!

(CARMELO starts to leave the magic circle. LILIA tries to hold him back, but she can't.)

LILIA: Come back to me—*please come back to meeeeeeee!!*

(CARMELO is out of the magic circle. He exits.)

(Alone, terrified, LILIA embraces herself and looks to the sky, crying openly.)

(Lights to normal daylight. We are back in the present reality. ALEGRIA, GUZMAN and MILTON look at the trembling LILIA.)

(LILIA sees the knife on the ground. She lunges at it, grabs it, and tries to stab herself in the heart.)

(MILTON runs to LILIA and grabs the knife away. She rages at him, slapping him, punching him—until she subsides. He embraces her gently. She buries her face in his chest and cries quietly.)

(End of Scene Six)

Scene Seven

(Continuous action)

(ALEGRIA and GUZMAN are on opposite sides of the stage. LILIA and MILTON are center. MILTON is holding her, stroking her hair.)

(LILIA slowly pulls away, wiping her eyes.)

MILTON: Are you all right?

(LILIA weakly nods yes. She stops crying. She looks at ALEGRIA.)

(ALEGRIA goes to LILIA and embraces her. She kisses him.)

(ALEGRIA collapses in her arms. He drops GUZMAN's watch. MILTON and LILIA hold up the weakened ALEGRIA.)

LILIA: *(To MILTON)* Can you take him home?

MILTON: *(To LILIA)* Are you going to be okay?

(As MILTON leads ALEGRIA to the house, ALEGRIA holds out his hand to GUZMAN.)

ALEGRIA: Guzman...I'm...

(GUZMAN spits at ALEGRIA's feet. MILTON and ALEGRIA exit.)

(Short silence)

(LILIA looks at GUZMAN's watch a long time. She picks it up, looking at it, thinking. He turns to her and tries to smile as if nothing happened.)

GUZMAN: I'm glad that's over. My ears are ringing. I'm a little shaky—must be hungry. *(No response from LILIA)* Why don't you go inside and make me something hot to eat? *(He sees the watch in her hands and smiles.)* Oh— look at this—my little girl! —*you have my watch!* —you little genius! I knew you wouldn't let me down! *¡Si, lo sabia! (He laughs and embraces LILIA. He lifts her up, spins her around, and kisses her. He puts her down.)* Give me the watch and things will go back to normal around this damn place! I'll show that son-of-a-bitch—.

(GUZMAN *holds out his hand.* LILIA *puts the watch on the ground. They look at each other.*)

GUZMAN: What are you doing? Give me the watch.

(LILIA *smashes the watch with her foot. The stage gets darker. The blow to the watch is a blow to* GUZMAN's *body. He covers his face with his hands, cries in pain, and looks at her, terrified. She looks at him with cold fury.*)

GUZMAN: Lilia, what are you doing…?

(LILIA *smashes the watch again, doubling* GUZMAN *over in pain. The stage gets darker. Another blow—darker—and he is brought to his knees.*)

GUZMAN: Lilia!

(*Another blow. Darker.* GUZMAN *is on the ground, crippled with pain.* LILIA *is on the brink of tears. He speaks out of pure desperation:*)

GUZMAN: I'm sorry your mother starved! I'm sorry Carmelo died! *I'm sorry*—.

(*Another blow. Almost black. Silence.* GUZMAN *is motionless, nearly dead.*)

GUZMAN: …Lilly, Lilly… *Sabes que te quiéro, por Dios….*

(LILIA *looks at* GUZMAN, *crying with hatred and pity. She raises her foot—and stops herself—unable to kill him.*)

(*She picks up the pieces of the watch and flings them into the air. Strange, wonderful lights fill the sky.*)

(*She runs into the house.*)

(*End of Scene Seven*)

Scene Eight

(Weeks later. The reddish light of an October afternoon.)

(GUZMAN is lying on stage, a beaten, blind old man.)

(MILTON enters. He is wearing a black sports jacket and black cowboy hat. He's carrying an attaché case, a walker, and dark sunglasses.)

(MILTON brings GUZMAN to his feet and makes him hold on to the walker. He puts the sunglasses on GUZMAN. GUZMAN is absolutely still, impaled, as it were, on the arms of the walker.)

(MILTON picks up the Virgin Mary and takes it offstage.)

(The bulldozer roars, very, very close.)

(MILTON reenters with a sign saying "No Trespassing. Property of the Mafia." He puts the sign over the porch. He looks at GUZMAN uncomfortably.)

MILTON: I saw Lolin and Hiberto at Alegria's funeral. They're getting married. *(Beat. No response.)* I took the Virgin Mary to the pawnbroker. Turns out she didn't come over from Spain during the Conquest, like you said. She came over from Japan, in the 1950s. She's worthless. *(Beat. No response.)* I also tried to get Malinche stuffed like you wanted. But the taxidermist couldn't get his knife through her. I tossed her in the pit. She's in hell, thank God.

(The bulldozer roars.)

MILTON: The governor of Puerto Rico called off the search for Marcario. No one's going to find those four hundred machetes, Pop. No one's going to free Puerto Rico.

(GUZMAN smiles. He doesn't have any emotional connection to what he's saying: His words come automatically.)

GUZMAN: ...Puerto Rico is like a little star next to the sun....

(The bulldozer roars. MILTON *pats his attaché case.)*

MILTON: Here's your book. "Tales of Marcario." I read your stories. I think they're really great. *(Embarrassed about lying to his father)* Well, actually, I don't—but listen. I want to take your book with me to Los Angeles. I want to sell these puppies to the studios. *(Pulls out a sheet of paper from his attaché case.)* This gives me the rights to your stories in perpetuity, throughout the universe. Sign here.

*(*MILTON *produces a pen and* GUZMAN *signs.)*

*(*LILIA *enters. She's dressed in black for* ALEGRIA's *funeral. Something has changed in her—she is wary but stronger, more in control of her fate. She looks at* MILTON *suspiciously.)*

LILIA: When you go to Hollywood, mister, you make sure Pop gets fifty percent of everything you make from those stories. Understand?

*(*MILTON *takes the contract and writes in it. The bulldozer roars.)*

MILTON: I'm off to the airport, Papi. Keep your eyes on the tube. Your stories are going to make this bad boy famous. *(To* LILIA:) Forty-nine percent?

LILIA: Goodbye Milton. Fifty.

*(*LILIA *and* MILTON *kiss—a long, warm embrace.* MILTON *kisses* GUZMAN *and exits, coughing loudly.)*

(Beat. LILIA *turns to* GUZMAN.)*

LILIA: I talked to the home. You're getting the one-bedroom on the first floor with the view of the woods. You'll like it. They serve rice and beans every Friday and have cockfights in the basement. All you have to do is go with me, and sign some papers.

GUZMAN: ...like a, like a, like a little star next to the sun...

(LILIA *turns away from* GUZMAN, *unable to look at him, trying to remain strong.*)

LILIA: I know what to do now. First, I'm going to get an education and a job. Then, someday, I'm going to have a baby. When I have that child—no matter whose it is or what it looks like—it's going to be Carmelo's child. In my dreams of Carmelo, I'm going to ask him to help raise our child. He's going to be a wonderful father! Then I'm never going to make love again. I'm going to be faithful to my husband as I promised him. *(She kisses her father and puts her gold cross around his neck.)* I'll visit you from time to time...that's what a daughter's supposed to do...but because you took away the man I love...I will make sure your grandchild will never know you, never know your stories, never pass the dreams and sorrows of our people to a new generation, as you wanted, Pop.

(Lights change. On the other side of the fence, the WOMAN *appears.)*

LILIA: I'm sorry, but you broke your promises to me. The ones you made before I was born—and after. A broken promise makes us free of each other. You set me free.

(The WOMAN *holds her burning heart out to* GUZMAN *and* LILIA.*)*

(We hear laughter: It's the haunting melancholy laugh of Elena we heard earlier. LILIA *smiles at the sound of her mother's voice. She exits.)*

*(*GUZMAN *hears the laughter and turns to look at the* WOMAN.*)*

(One by one, the husks of corn begin to bleed. Lights up to intense white as the trickle of blood becomes a torrent. Hold tableau. Down to black)

END OF PLAY